THIS ISSUE OF PURATATTVA IS PUBLISHED ON THE OCCASION OF THE SILVER JUBILEE CELEBRATIONS OF THE NATIONAL MUSEUM, NEW DELHI (1985-86).

पुरातत्त्व
PURĀTATTVA

Bulletin of the Indian Archaeological Society

No. 15 1984-85

Editor
S.P. Gupta

D.K. Printworld (P) Ltd.
New Delhi

Cataloging in Publication Data — DK
[Courtesy : D.K. Agencies (P) Ltd. <docinfo@dkagencies.com>]

Purātattva : bulletin of the Indian Archaeological Society, no. 15, 1984-85 / editor, S.P. Gupta.
p. cm.
Includes bibliographical references.
ISBN 8124602905

1. Archaeology — India — Periodicals. 2. India — Antiquities — Periodicals. 3. India — Civilization — Periodicals. I. Gupta, S.P. (Swarajya Prakash), 1931 - II. Indian Archaeological Society.

DDC 934 21

First Published in 1986
First Reprinted in 2005
ISBN 81-246-0290-5
Price for volume 15 (1984-85): Rs. 800 US $ 40

Reprint authorised by
Indian Archaeological Society
New Delhi - 110 016

The Editors are not responsible for the opinions expressed by the Contributors.

Purātattva is published annually.

Manuscripts (whether in the form of articles or notes or book reviews) offered for publication should be sent to the Editor, Purātattva, Indian Archaeological Society, B-17, Qutab Institutional Area, New Delhi - 110 016.

Published and printed by:
D.K. Printworld (P) Ltd.
'Srikunj,' F-52, Bali Nagar
New Delhi – 110015
Phone : (011) 2545 3975, 2546 6019 Fax : (011) 2546 5926
E-mail : dkprintworld@vsnl.net
www. dkprintworld.com

PURATATTVA

NUMBER 15, 1984-85

CONTENTS

NOTES AND NEWS

BOOK REVIEWS

PURATATTVA

NUMBER 15 1984-85

EDITORIAL

The year 1985 is a landmark in the history of the Indian Archaeological Society. The land offered to the Society by the Delhi Development Authority (B-17, Institutional Land, south of IIT, near Jawaharlal Nehru University) to establish a Centre for Research and Training in History, Archaeology and Palaeo-environment was finally acquired and registered. As a follow up action, M/s Sharat Dass and Associates, a highly reputed Delhi based firm of architects, who designed the Indira Gandhi Stadium, were selected, after an open competition through newspaper advertisement, and awarded the contract of designing and making the architectural drawings, etc. The conceptual drawings are ready. The Foundation stone of the Centre will be laid during the eighteenth annual conference of the Society to be held at New Delhi in January 1986. This most solemn act will be performed by Dr. D.P. Singhal, Professor of History, Queensland University, Brisbane, Australia on the 5th January, 1986. Happily, on this occasion Dr. A.K. Narain, Professor of Indian History at the Wisconsin University, USA, who founded the Indian Archaeological Society in 1967 at Varanasi, will also be present along with Prof. B.B. Lal, Fellow, Indian Institute of Advanced Studies, Simla, who has been crusading for such a Centre for more than a decade now. Dr. Devahuti, Professor of History, Delhi University, Delhi and her husband, made available rupees 11.5 lakhs (realized through the sale proceeds of a residential land) to the Society for this purpose. She has been, and is still, planning this Centre with meticulous care. Last year, during the seventeenth annual conference of the Society held at Guwahati, Assam, under the chairpersonship of Prof. Devahuti, a committee was formed to formulate a constitution of the proposed Centre. This has been done and the draft constitution will be presented to the General Body of the Society for disscussion and adoption.

We thank Sarvashri K.S. Ramachandran, S. Ganesh Rao, Sudhakar Sharma, Jitendra Kumar, Dr.Shashi Asthana Dr. K.P. Shankar for seeing this issue of the *Puratattva* through the press.

We take this opportunity to thank the Director, National Museum, New Delhi, and the Department of Culture, Ministry of Human Resources Development, Government of India, for inviting and hosting the annual conference of the Society along with two other societies — Indian History and Culture Society and Indian Society for Prehistoric and Quaternary Studies — as an important event of the Silver Jubilee Celebrations of the National Museum (1985-86).

New Delhi

S.P. Gupta

27-12-85.

MESOLITHIC HUMAN REMAINS FROM THE GANGETIC PLAIN SARAI NAHAR RAI

Kenneth A.R. Kennedy, Christopher B. Burrow, and Nancy C. Lovell

INTRODUCTION

Discovered in 1968, the site of Sarai Nahar Rai in the Gangetic Plain is important to palaeoanthropologists both for its archaeological record of Mesolithic artifacts and associated faunal remains, and for its mortuary series of fifteen human skeletons. This is one of the largest skeletal series of Mesolithic hominids from India discovered to date, and the condition of preservation of the remains is unusually good. Advanced mineralization of the bones, in undisturbed burial deposits, has allowed for the recovery of a number of relatively complete skulls and postcranial bones. All of the skeletal specimens are adults, thus permitting their morphometric analysis and comparison with other prehistoric skeletal series of adult specimens.

The excavation in 1978-1979 of thirty-five well-preserved fossil hominid skeletons from Mahadaha, a Mesolithic site 50 km from Sarai Nahar Rai, allows an unparalleled opportunity for morphometric and statistical studies of two adjacent, and perhaps contemporary, populations of the Mesolithic period in the valley of the Ganga. The site has faunal and cultural components similar to those found at Sarai Nahar Rai. The Mahadaha skeletal series has been examined by the senior author, and will be reported in Part II of this publication. The authors welcome the opportunity, provided by the Indian Archaeological Society, to offer to scholars the results of research conducted in 1980 at the Allahabad University.

HISTORICAL BACKGROUND OF RESEARCH

More than a century has passed since the initial discovery of human skeletal remains from Mesolithic cultural contexts in India. However, laboratory examinations and comparative morphometric analysis were never made on the skeletons observed by Carlleyle (1883, 1885; Allchin 1958) at Mahara Pahar, Uttar Pradesh, in 1880-1881, nor on a skull uncovered a decade later by Foote (1916) at Jalampura, Gujarat, nor on human remains collected by Hunter (1935, 1936) in the 1930s, from Pachmarhi, Madhya Pradesh. Serious study of the skeletal biology of Mesolithic peoples in India did not get underway until forty-five years ago with the excavations at Langhnaj, Gujarat, by Sankalia and his associates (Ehrhardt and Kennedy 1965; Karve-Corvinus and Kennedy 1964; Sankalia and Karve 1949). Since 1941, additional Mesolithic skeletons have been recovered and examined, with important collections coming from Bagor, Rajasthan, in 1968-1970 (Lukacs *et al.* 1982; Misra 1976) and from Bhimbetka, Madhya Pradesh, since 1971 (Kennedy *et al.* MS, in press; Misra *et al.* 1977; Wakankar 1975). Especially significant are the discoveries made, since 1963, by archaeological teams directed by G.R. Sharma at Mesolithic sites of the Kaimur hills and Ganga valley in Uttar Pradesh. The Kaimur rockshelter of Lekhahia ki Pahari has yielded nineteen skeletons, and a single specimen found at Baghai Khor rockshelter has now been examined by Kennedy and Burrow (Sharma 1965, 1973). Other Mesolithic burials have been observed at Harli-Bhituli and Karka in the lake country of the Ganga valley.

Mesolithic sites with human skeletal remains extend into island Sri Lanka. In 1939, P. E. P. Deraniyagala excavated specimens from the cave of Batadomba lena, Sabaragamuva Province, in an archaeological context that was called the *Balagoda culture* (the *Bandarawelian* culture of Noone and Noone 1940). Additional burials were recovered from the cave of Ravan Alla, Uva Province, in 1945, and from the cave of Alu Galge in the same province in 1954. Fifteen human skeletons were collected from the open air site of Bellanbandi Palassa, Sabaragamuva, which was discovered in 1956 and excavated in 1957, 1961 and 1970. The Sri Lankan sites have been discussed in works by P.E.P. Deraniyagala (1963) and S.U. Deraniyagala (1981) and a descrip tion of the human skeletons from Bellanbandi Palassa has also been published (Kennedy 1965). Since 1978, S.U. Deraniyagala has recovered human skeletons in Mesolithic cultural contexts at the cave of Beli lena, Kitulgala, and at Batadomba lena. Radiocarbon dating of samples from the skeletal-bearing deposits are *circa* 16,000 years b.p. for Batadomba lena and *circa* 12,500 years b.p. for Beli lena. A description of the remains of twenty-seven individuals from the two sites has been published (Kennedy *et al.* 1985). Sri Lanka has provided palaeoanthropologists with the earliest fossils of *Homo sapiens sapiens* recovered thus far in South Asia, and these have significant implications for the later Mesolithic and skeletal deposits at Sarai Nahar Rai and Mahadaha.

Pakistan has not provided a human skeletal record of Mesolithic association, nor have human remains of this cultural horizon been recovered from archaeological sites in eastern and peninsular India. A catalogue of South Asian Prehistoric human skeletal remains and burial practices, including Mesolithic specimens, is now available (Kennedy and Caldwell 1984), and a preliminary description of the Sarai Nahar Rai and Mahadaha specimens is already in print (Kennedy 1984a).

Although Sarai Nahar Rai was discovered in 1968, its excavation did not commence until four years later. Eight skeletons were removed, and, in 1973, six more skeletons were recovered. The significance of the human remains from Sarai Nahar Rai was appreciated immediately by Dr. P. C. Dutta and his affiliates of the Anthropological Survey of India, who removed one skeleton in 1970. Their published reports began to appear as early as 1971 (Dutta 1971, 1973; Dutta and Pal 1972; Dutta *et al.* 1971; Dutta *et al.* 1972), and a photograph of the cranium from the first excavated skeleton appeared in *Nature* that year (Dutta 1971). A recent re-study by Dutta (1984) of the Sarai Nahar Rai specimen retained at the Anthropological Survey of India, Calcutta, provides new morphometric data and collates valuable information on the geology, climate, fauna, vegetation and associated artifacts from the site. The earliest announcements of the Sarai Nahar Rai remains have engendered certain ideas about the nature and biological affinities of the population, ideas which must be reconsidered and evaluated in the light of the present study, which has incorporated most of the specimens removed from the site. This study favours a palaeodemographic orientation, rather than one focused upon racial palaeontology.

Apart from announcements in *Indian Archaeology — A Review* (1969-1970), and a more detailed study in the *Journal of the Indian Anthropological Society* (Dutta *et al.* 1971) and in *Disposal of the Dead and Physical Types in Ancient India* (Gupta 1972), archaeological reports of the site and its burials were not published until 1973 and 1975 (Sharma 1973, 1975). The 1973 summary report includes a discussion of preservation and completeness of the skeletons which had been recovered the previous year, along with a description of cultural materials found in the graves. In that report, the skeletons collected in 1972 are identified by the catalogue numbers I, II, III, IV, V, IX, X and XIII. To this series was added the six additional skeletons collected during the 1973 excavation season. These bear Roman numeral catalogue numbers as well and are distinguished from the 1972 series by prefacing the specimen number with its appropriate date, e.g., Skeleton 1972-III and Skeleton 1973-III. Of this total fourteen skeletons, nine are suitable for morphometric analysis. There is one additional skeleton which is suitable for morphological analysis only. The remaining four skeletons not included in this study were either absent from the existing Sarai Nahar Rai series at Allahabad University, or were too fragmentary to merit morphometric analysis. One of these, Skeletons 1973—IV, is still embedded in solidified soil matrix, and retained in this form as a display specimen in the museum of the Department of Ancient History, Culture and Archaeology at Allahabad University. The senior author, with the assistance of Mr. C. B. Burrow, studied the Sarai Nahar Rai skeletal series in the autumn of 1980 at the Department of Ancient History, Culture and Archaeology, Allahabad University. Two of the studied skeletons (1972—III, a male, and 1973—III, a female) are currently displayed in a glass case in the museum of this department, alongside two other adult skeletons and three skulls from Mahadaha. This exhibit, and a poster description of the major biological characteristics of the Sarai Nahar Rai and Mahadaha skeletal series, was prepared by the senior and second authors on the occasion of the Silver Jubilee Celebration of the department in November 1980, at the request of G. R. Sharma. The skeleton removed from Sarai Nahar Rai in 1970 is housed now at the headquarters of the Anthropological Survey of India, Calcutta, where it was examined by the senior and second authors upon completion of their research of the series retained in Allahabad. This specimen bears the catalogue number 1970 — IV, and is included in the present study.

The problem of the chronology of the Mesolithic in India is a complex one. Consequently, in an attempt of facilitate the evaluation and comparison of radiocarbon dates for several sites, we have turned to the original publications of radiocarbon date lists, and have adopted current conventions in the report of these dates. All dates are reported in this paper in radiocarbon years b.p. (before present), present being defined as A.D. 1950. Since 1976, radiocarbon dates are no longer converted to B.C./A.D. calendar years simply by subtracting 1950 from the radiocarbon years. Instead, the radiocrabon year date, b.p., must first be converted to calendar years, B.P., by the application of a calibration curve, and then the 1950 may be subtracted. Conventional radiocarbon dates need to be calibrated because of temporal variations in the amount of radiocarbon in the atmosphere. Many different calibration curves have been produced over the years, and their diversity of results has resulted in a suspicion of calibration on the part of many archaeologists. However, a reasonable consensus of opinion has now been reached by many of the world's radiocarbon laboratories, and we recommend that readers adopt the calibration strategy advanced by Klein *et al.* (1982). Their published tables permit one to take a date in radiocarbon years, with its associated uncertainty, and obtain a 95% confidence interval containing the 'true' calendric date. Calibrations are included back more than 7,000 years, making them relevant for the Indian Mesolithic.

In the interests of ease of comparison, all dates reported here are uncalibrated. Readers should be aware, however, that other publications may report calibrated dates. These should cite the calibration curve used. If published prior to 1976, many publications gave uncalibrated dates, so care must be taken when comparing radiocarbon dates from different publications.

THE SITE OF SARAI NAHAR RAI

Sarai Nahar Rai (81 degrees 51 minutes East Long., 25 degrees 48 minutes North Lat.) is 15 km southwest of Pratapgarh town in Pratapgarh pargana, Uttar Pradesh (Line Drawing 1, Figure 1). This is within the central Ganga valley. This region is bounded on the south by the Ganga river and on the north by the Sarju river. The site is situated on the shore of an ancient oxbow lake, an isolated meander of the Ganga of terminal Pleistocene times. The river's present course is 55 km

Map of Sarai Nahar Rai and Other Prehistoric Sites Mentioned in the Text.

Figure 1. Site of Sarai Nahar Rai.

to the south. The lake is now dry, save for a small vestige 4.5 km to the west at Srinagar village where it is known as Khoalan jhil. However, when the lake bed held water for most of the year, its shore provided an open-air camp and burial ground used by nomadic hunter-gatherer bands of Mesolithic people. The total area which retains traces of their occupancy measures 2800 m^2 and is marked by microliths, hearths, faunal remains and burials which are exposed in the severely eroded eastern part of the site.

The soil of the region is saline, yellow or whitish in colour, with heavy calcium content (carbonate of lime nodules and black kankar), and includes a compact black soil which is the trace of the old lake deposit proper. The Gangetic alluvium forms a relatively flat topography with an average altitude of 915 m above sea level. Salt abounds in the area. In his geological and topographical description of Sarai Nahar Rai, Dutta (1984: 37-40) notes that the area of the site is well wooded and drained by the Sai river and its affluents. One of these, the Belkhari Nahar, flows within 1 km of the north-east limit of the ancient occupation area. Underlying the younger Gangetic alluvium of sand, silt, and clay is an older alluvium, rich in deposits of calcium carbonate in the form of kankars (nodules), particularly in the *usar* tracts. *Reh,* a saline product, also occurs in these soils. Interment of the skeletons in this hard pan of lime concretions explains certain factors of their condition of preservation and mineralization. The reader is urged to consult Dutta's valuable study for a more detailed account of the pedocalic soil horizon at Sarai Nahar Rai, and its context in the broader stratigraphic picture of this part of the Gangetic Plain.

Sharma (1973) classified the cultural associations of Sarai Nahar Rai as belonging to a geometric microlithic horizon of the early Mesolithic, a tradition characterized in this part of South Asia by small and finely retouched stone tools, such as symmetrical points, lunates, blunted-back blades, scrapers, and triangles. These were fabricated on chalcedony carnelian or other fine-grained stones. Large tools are essentially absent. Points and blades predominate over puncturing-boring tools and arrowhead. Nongeometric microliths are present in high frequency. Small clay vessels, made by hand with the coiling technique, were found in most of the graves.

Faunal remains are fragmentary, and are most often encountered in hearths, with microliths. Some of the bones are charred. Sharma (1975) has identified the mammals as *Bos indicus, Bos bubulis, Ovis* sp., *Capra* sp., and *Elephas indicus.* This represents a small proportion of the mammals living in the Ganga-Yumuna region at the end of the Pleistocene, which included *Equus onager khur, Elephas maximus, Bos gaurus, Gazella* sp., *Antelope* sp., *Cervus* sp., *Canis* sp., *Hystrix* sp., and *Mus* (Dutta 1984: 39; Dassarma and Biswas 1976). Remains of fish and tortoise are also found. Pollen analysis, of a sample collected from a 3.30m deep deposit from an oxbow lake in the vicinity of the site, was conducted by Gupta (1976). Results suggest the presence of open grasslands with low tree cover at the time of occupation of Sarai Nahar Rai, followed by a period of greater tree cover. These are conditions which characterize the onset of more arid conditions at the termination of the Pleistocene, as the Gangetic Plain gained pedocalic soil cover and greater salinity.

The human burials occurred in shallow oblong graves, which had been dug into the hard soil of the habitation area. Some specimens had been exposed by erosion before the discovery of the site. Skeletons were found in an extended supine position, and oriented east-west with the skulls to the west. Both single and multiple graves were found. One grave contained four individuals buried at the same time, with two males placed to the right side of two females. There were no infant, child, or early adolescent burials (Figures 2 and 3).

An uncalibrated radiocarbon date of 10,500 $\pm$ 110 years b.p. was obtained from a sample of

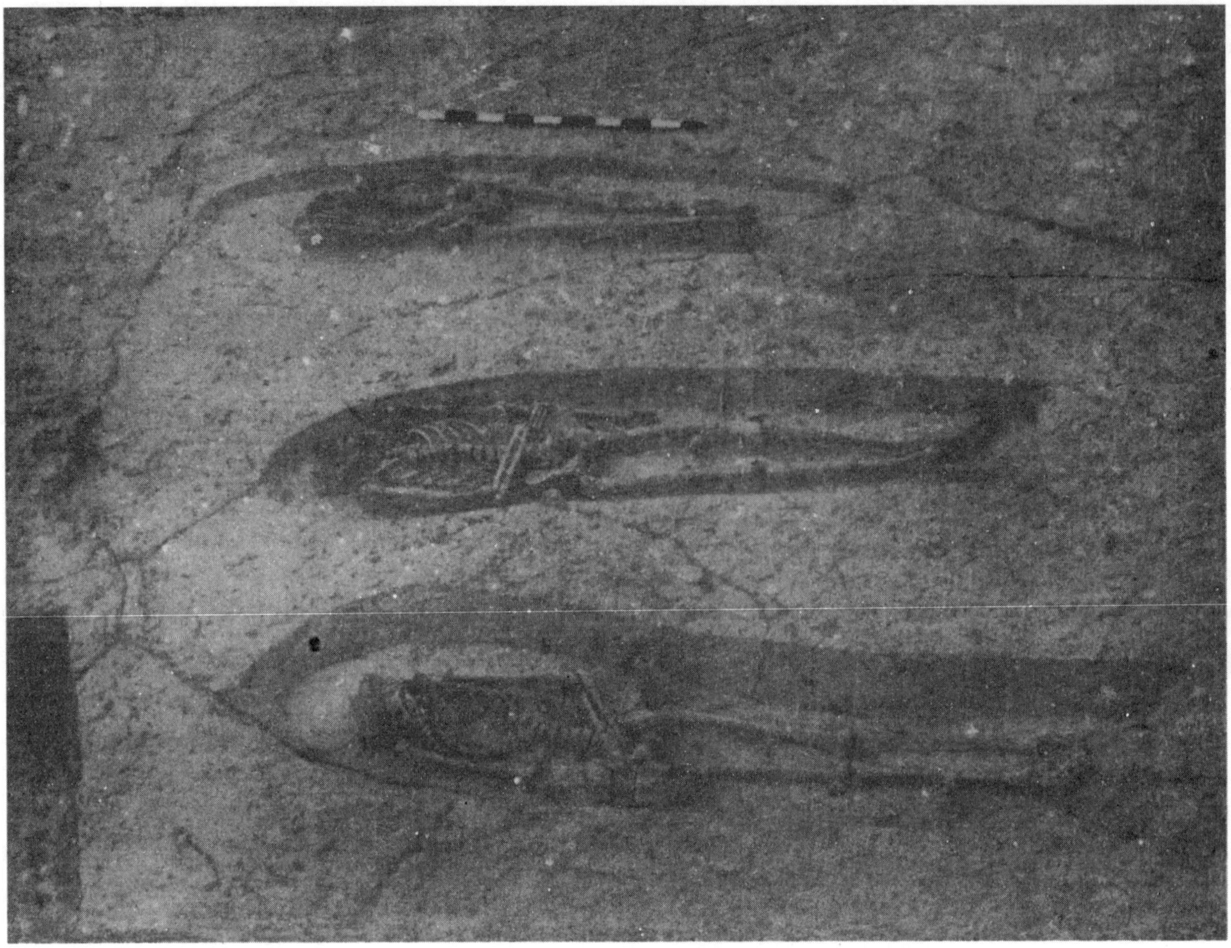

Figure 2. Skeletons 1972-XIII (lower), 1972-X (middle), and 1972-IX (upper), in situ.

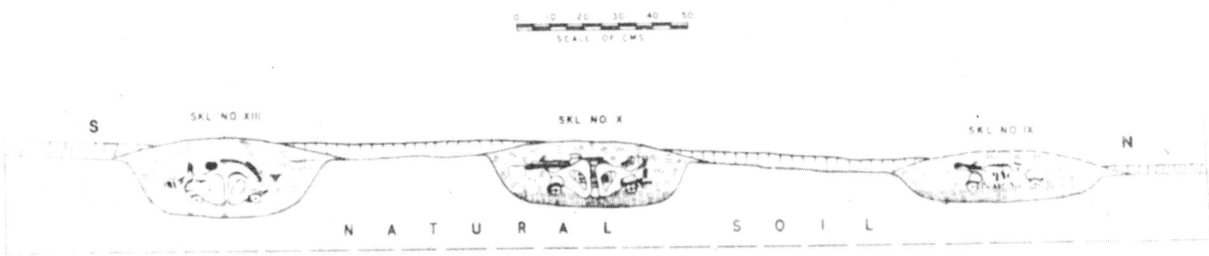

Figure 3. Section across graves of Skeleton 1972-IX, 1972-X, and 1972-XIII.

unburnt, highly clacified, human bone (Agrawal and Kusumgar 1973). This date may be considered unreliable, since it was obtained on the inorganic matrix of unburnt bone. Although the issue is not settled, many researchers consider the inorganic carbon to be highly susceptible to contamination by carbon exchange with groundwater (Aitken 1974; Michels 1973; Tite 1972). It should also be noted that a much younger radiocarbon date of 2,860 ± 120 b.p. (Agrawal and Kusumgar 1975), made on charred bones, considered to be less susceptible to contamination of the inorganic matrix (Ralph 1971), has also been obtained. Currently, radiocarbon measurements made on the organic portions of bone (collagen) and shell (conchiolin) are viewed as the most reliable, since the covalent bonding of the organic matrix does not appear to permit carbon exchange with the burial environment.

The nearby Mesolithic site of Mahagara has rendered radiocarbon dates of 9,830 ± 160 b,p., and 11,550 ± 180 b.p. (Rajagopalan *et al.*1982), and 10,980 ± 190 b.p. and 13,740 ± 380 b.p. (Agrawal *et al.* 1985). Unfortunately, these dates were made on the inorganic portion of shell, which is also susceptible to contamination. The lack of overlap between these dates, and a younger date of 3,300 ± 100 b.p. (Rajagopalan *et al.* 1982), obtained on usually reliable charcoal, reinforces the suggestion that those older dates may be unreliable. However, the type of pedocalic soil in which the skeletons of Sarai Nahar Rai were buried was developed at the onset of the Holocene, according to Dutta (1984: 49). Certainly, on the basis of Oakley's (1964: 4-5) Fourth Order Relative Dating procedures, the skeletal specimens are in harmony with what palaeoanthropologists expect to encounter, with respect to a suite of anatomical features, in terminal Pleistocene-Early Holocene deposits in other parts of the world. A comparison of radiocarbon dates for Sarai Nahar Rai and other Mesolithic sites with skeletons, such as Bagor in Rajasthan, Lekhahia ki Pahari in Uttar Pradesh, and Langhnaj in Gujarat, is presented in Table I. It is appartent from the great diversity of dates that the evidence for the antiquity of the Indian Mesolithic is presently inconclusive.

CONDITION OF PRESERVATION OF SKELETAL SPECIMENS

The condition of preservation and the number of indentifiable human bones present at Sarai Nahar Rai in 1972 are among the data included in Sahrma's (1973: 135-138) published account of the Mesolithic cultures of the Ganga valley. Individual bone identification in the field was made by V. D. Misra and A. Pal who supervised the lifting of the skeletons. Their report is confirmed by an extensive photographic record of the burials, *in situ* and during the process of excavation. These were examined by us at the time of our analysis of the sketetons, which had been transported in the interim to Allahabad University. With some minor exceptions, our osteological indentifications correspond with those of the archaeological investigators, although certain bones had been removed, and the transport of sketetons from the site to the research institution resulted in some inevitable, but fortunately minimal, damage. Indeed, we were most favourably impressed with the care accorded these human remains with respect to the recording of data and the packing of bones for storage. The same high standards of curatorship were maintained in the 1973 excavation season at Sarai Nahar Rai.

Some cleaning and restoration of bones had been attempted at the site, but the initial taks of the present investigators was the thorough cleaning and reconstruction of the bulk of the collection. Cleaning involved removal of loose soil, extraction of the hard calcareous matrix, and separation of bones adhering together with the soil or calcareous matrix serving as a bonding agent. Reconstruction involved mending bones, which had fractured before, during, or after excavation, where breaks had occuredd with clean margins. No attempt was made to correct distortion such as warping of skull bones, caused by erosional forces. However, these modifications were given appropriate consideration in the secondary phase of laboratory analysis— the metrical and morphological examination.

Bones of the Sarai Nahar Rai skeletal series have undergone considerable fossilization. Most of the large bones are heavier than recnetly macerated bones, and have a metallic ring when tapped with a hard instrument. In addition to the high mineral component in the compact and cancellous bone tissues, there are varying degress of mineral concretions deposited over the external surfaces of many bones.

This form of preservation allowed the skeletons to remain relatively intact despite their exposure by erosion. Dentition, when present, is well preserved. Nitrogen and Fluorine assays, if conducted to determine the ratio of inorganic to organic constituents of the bones, as well as to establish the amount of Fluorine absorbed from groundwater, would provide a quantitative index of the degree of fossilization, as well as a measure of the degree of contemporaneity of the burials themselves and their temporal relationships to the associated faunal remains.

The degree of preservation and completeness of each part of the skeleton observed in the laboratory are summarized in Table II. The categories of *Complete* (C), *Incomplete* (I), and *Fragmentary* (F) are relative, but if a part of the skeleton of an individual is *Missing* (-------), this denotes that the part was not observed in the laboratory. A missing bone may appear in a site record or photograph but not be available in the laboratory setting for any number of reasons. The category C is applied when a large number of metrical and morphological observations can be made because the major portion of a skeletal component is present. This symbol applies when a skeletal specimen has retained a complete skull or a complete femur. When a skeletal component yields relatively less quantitative and qualitative data because of postmortem damage, yet still allows for some significant analysis, it is identified as I. For example, a femur may have retained its diaphysis and proximal end but its distal end is missing: such a bone is classified as I in Table II. This same category has been assigned to the bones of the hand and foot when some components of these members are missing or are severely damaged. Skeletal remains yielding minimal morphometric data because of postmortem damage are labelled F, and these may include splinters or small segments of bones.

MORPHOMETRIC ANALYSIS

Methodology

Calibrations are based upon methods described in the third edition of Martin and Saller's (1957) *Lehrbuch für Anthropologie.* Each standard used in the present study is identified by its code number, which is placed adjacent to the name of the measurement in Tables III, IV and V. Measurements of Molar Tooth Row Length and Premolar-Tooth Row Length, for the maxillary and mandibular dentitions, are not accompanied by a Martin and Saller code number. These measurements are taken with the sliding caliper, graduated at 1 mm units, and are the straight line distance measured from the mesial border of the first molar (or premolar) to the distal border of the third molar. Mid-shaft circumferences of the long bones are measured with a steel metric tape, which is placed against the bone at the middle portion of the diaphysis, pulled tight, and the reading taken at the point of intersection of the tape as it encircles the shaft.

Instruments used for quantitative data include the Seiber-Hegner/Gestetner sliding and spreading calipers graduated to 0.05 mm units, and the mandibular goniometer and palatometer graduated to 1.0 mm units. An osteometric board was constructed in the laboratory with graph paper lined in 1.0 mm units. All measurements are given to $\pm$ 1 mm. The manufacturer of the mandibular goniometer and palatometer is the Una Company. The authors' photographic record was taken with the Olympia camera, model OM-2, with 50 mm and macro lens attachments, and with film speed of 400 ASA for black and white exposures. All photographs of the specimens *in situ* from the archaeological site itself are the property of the Department of Ancient History, Culture and Archaeology, Allahabad University. One procedure for age determination utilized the set of standard bone models of the pubic symphyses, as defined and classified by McKern and Stewart (1957), and Gilbert and McKern (1973). The Hanna and Washburn (1953) determination of sex of skeletons, by means of an Ischial-Pubic Index, has been used in this study along with other procedures for estimation of sex. Stature estimations were based upon calculations from lengths of long bones of the upper and lower extremities as formulated by Trotter (1970). For both age and stature estimations the tables for white (Caucasian) males and females were consulted.

DESCRIPTION OF SPECIMENS

Skeleton 1972-I

This very fragmentary specimen is represented entirely by postcranial bones. These are poorly preserved. Of the bones of the thorax, the sacrum is in three pieces, and, when articulated, these reveal a slight degree of concavity of the anterior surfaces of the sacral bodies. A right humerus fragment, found with the sacrum, is a non-human bone. Fragments of the right radius and right ulna show moderate degrees of muscular development of the interosseous lines. There is incomplete ossification of the proximal epiphysis of the third metacarpal bone with its diaphysis. A fragmented portion of the left innominate has a relatively narrow sciatic notch. The two femora have a moderate degree of robusticity. The angle of the collo-diaphysial junction of the right femur falls within the metrical value for males. From these data it is concluded that this is a male of 16 to 18 years of age at time of death. No pathological or anomalous features are observed.

Skeletons 1973-II (Figure 11)

The mandible is represented by the right corpus and gonial portion of the ramus, but alveolar portions and dentition are missing. Th. gonium is sharply everted and supports prominent attachments for the right Pterygoid muscle. The mental eminence is bilateral in form.

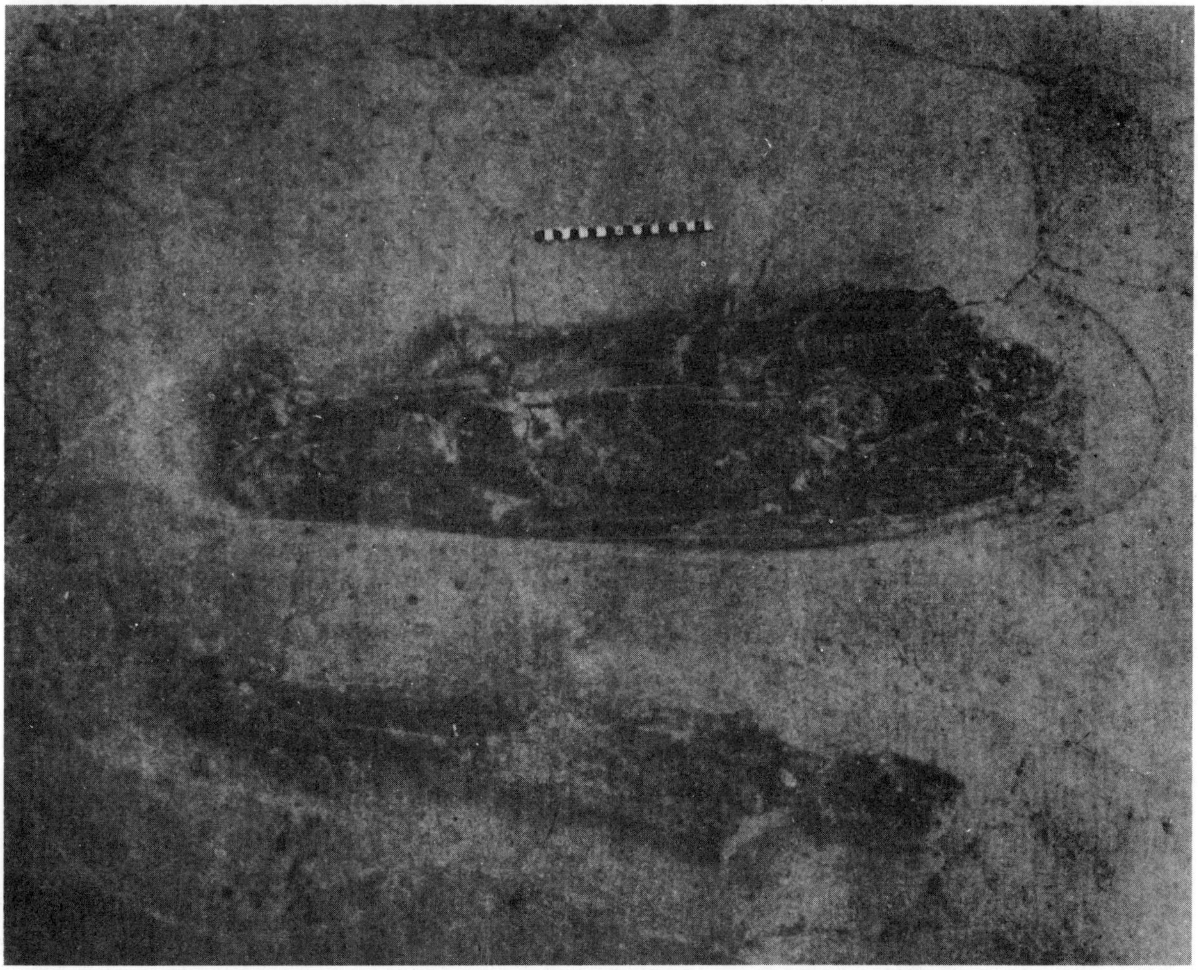

Figure 11. Skeletons 1973-II (lower) and 1973-III (upper), in situ.

Of the thoracic bones, the sternum has a manubrium of slight robusticity with a jugular notch of moderate depth, and an incompletely fused corpus of five segments. The sacrum is hyperbasal, and curvature of its anterior surface commences just inferior to the third sacral body. The first and second sacral bodies remain unfused. The lumbar and thoracic vertebrae exhibit slight lipping on the articular surfaces of the bodies, an interesting feature given the young age of this individual. Of the bones of the pectoral girdle, the clavicles are remarkable for their large size and pronounced muscular development, the right clavicle being the more robust of the pair. The scapulae are large and robust also, with massive acromial processes and the shallow glenoid cavities which are devoid of any lipping. Upper extremities are marked by large humeri, with a distinct bicipital groove on the right humerus. Radii are flat, rather than elevated, in the tuberosity for Deltoid attachment. Sharp interosseous lines appear on both ulnae. Both humeri and radii are slightly bowed. Hand bones are large, and their epihysial union is complete. While fragmentary, the innominates have preserved their sciatic nothches, which are intermediate in morphology to the norms for male and feamle pelvic bones. However, there are no preauricular sulci, and muscular development of the iliac crests indicate maleness. Arcuate lines are broad, dull and mound-shaped. Other male features are observed in the large and high linea aspera and pilasters of the right femur, and the pronounced development of the lesser trochanter. The tibiae have massive tuberosities, and, like the femur, are absolutely large in size. There is little retroversion of the proximal end of the tibiae, and the shafts are straight. Squatting facets are prominent on the distal ends of both tibiae. The fibulae are not especially robust or deeply fluted. These bones, and the bones of the foot, show completed epiphysial union. As noted above, there is some lipping of the vertebral bodies: a similar degree of lipping appears on the patellae, along the posterior surfaces of the lateral and inferior borders, and at the apex of the superior borders, where it is most pronounced. The condition is worse on the left knee and suggests a generalized exostosis, related perhaps to a chronic but low level inflammation of the joint.

The morphological features noted here support the decision that this is a male specimen. The estimate of age is based upon interpretation of the left pubic symphysis for which the sum of the three components is 6 on the McKern and Stewart (1957) models. This suggests an age of 20 to 24 years with a mean age of 22.42 ± 0.99 years.

Skeleton 1972 -III (Figures 4-10)

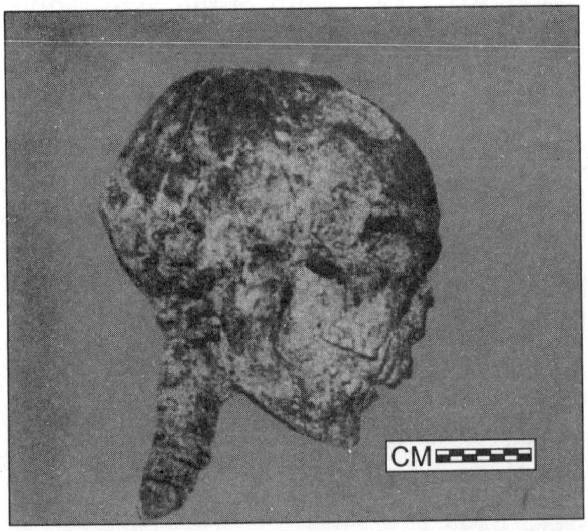

Figure 4. Skeleton 1972-III in situ.

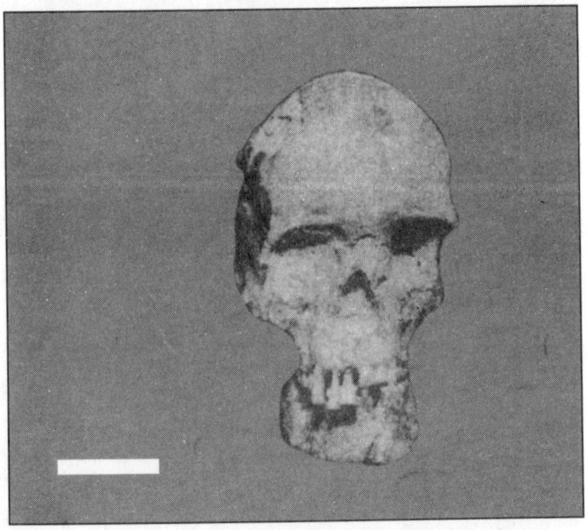

Figure 5. Skull of Sarai Nahar Rai – Specimen 1972-III, frontal aspect.

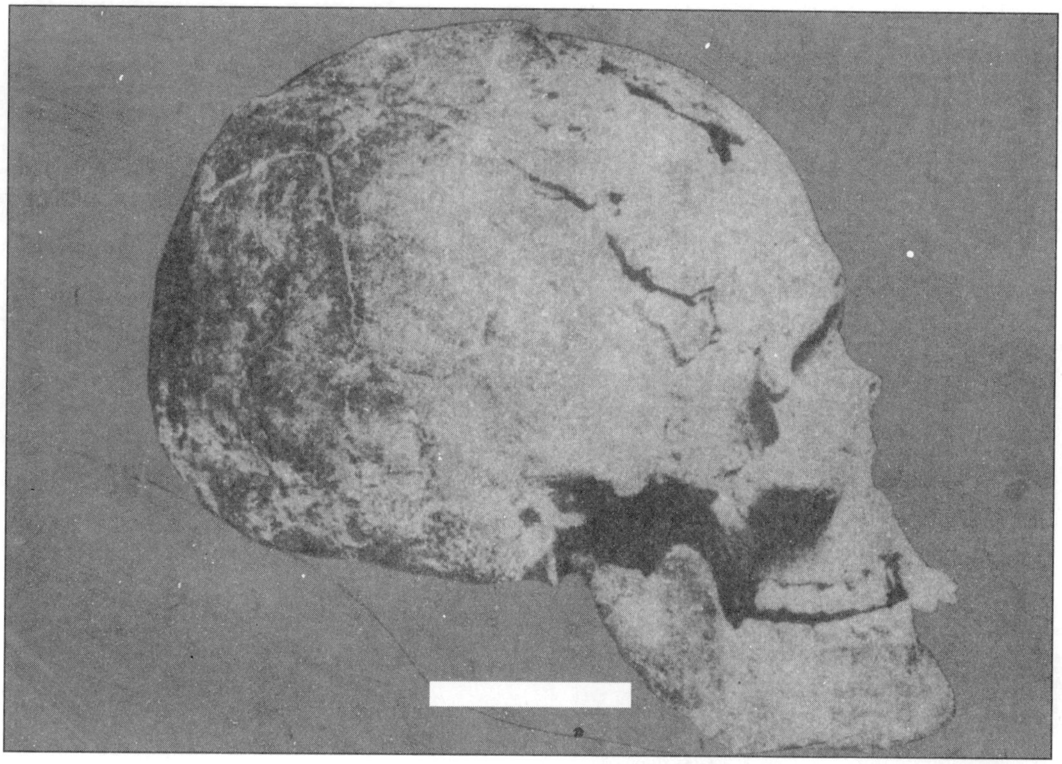

Figure 6. Skull of Sarai Nahar Rai – Specimen 1972-III, right lateral aspect.

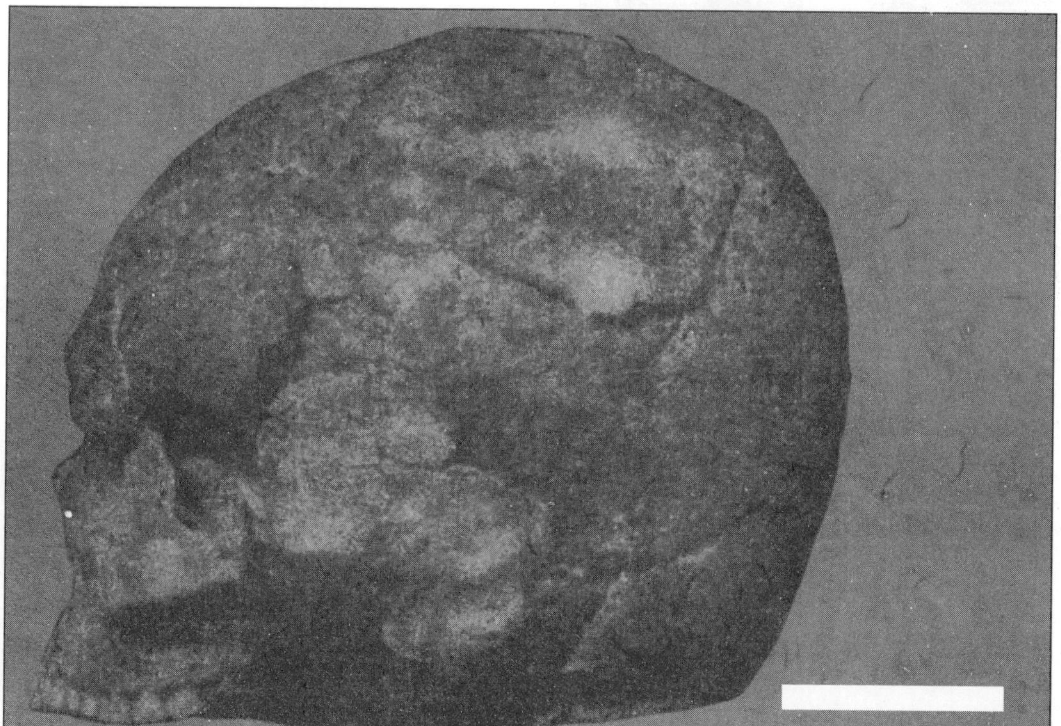

Figure 7. Skull of Sarai Nahar Rai – Specimen 1972-III, left lateral aspect.

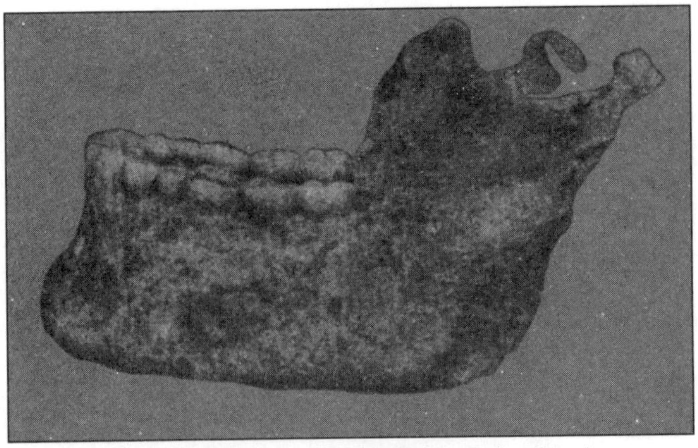

Figure 9. Mandible of Sarai Nahar Rai – Specimen 1972-III, left lateral aspect.

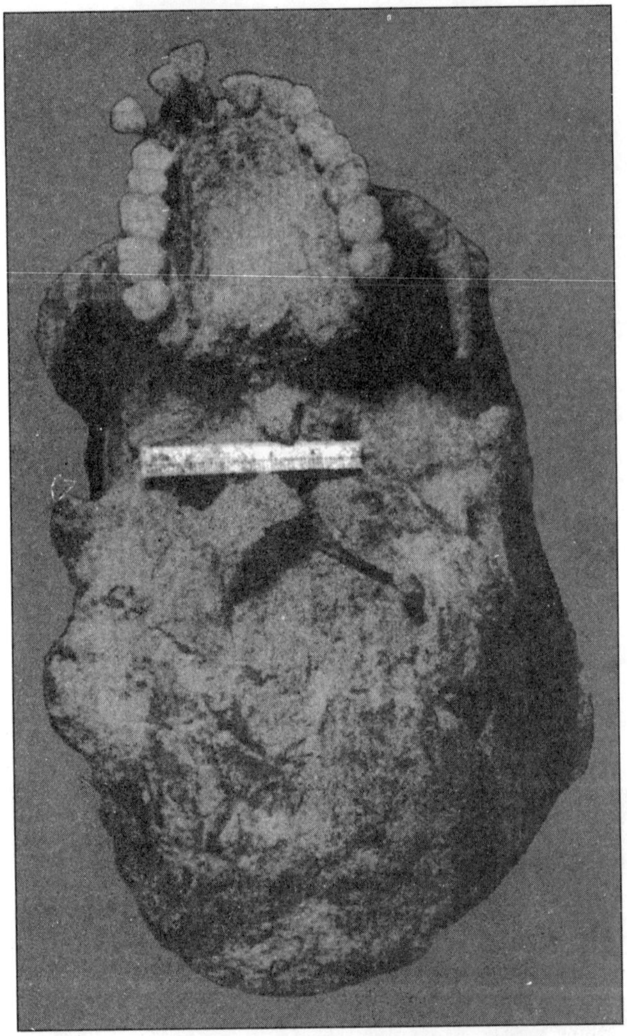

Figure 8. Cranium of Sarai Nahar Rai – Specimen 1972-III, basalar aspect.

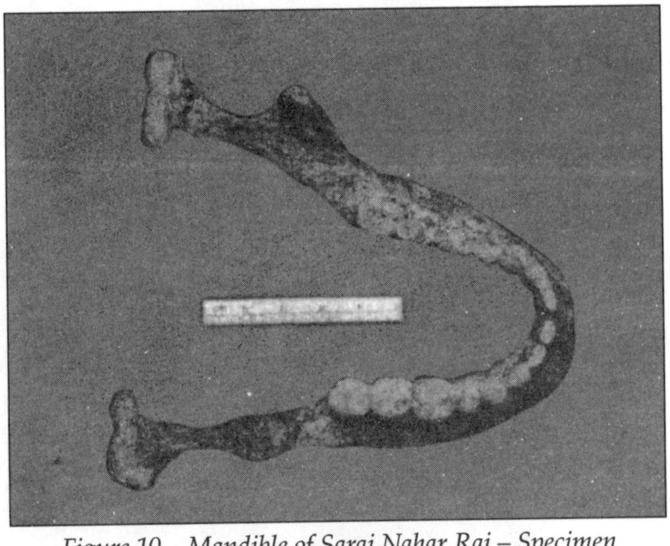

Figure 10. Mandible of Sarai Nahar Rai – Specimen 1972-III, superior aspect.

The skull of this specimens is almost complete. However, the cranial vault has been crushed severely, resulting in some distortion to the right side. The face is also skewed to the right, and is slightly compressed. While these postmortem deformations preclude the taking of certain measurements, it is apparent from other measurements that the cranial vault is hyperdolichocranic and tapeinocranic. As a whole, the skull is large and robust, its muscularity appearing most obviously in the sharp temporal lines, deep digastric fossae of the mastoid region, and large supramastoid crests. The frontal bone supports a moderately pronounced supraorbital torus which is of bilateral form, a large glabella, and a deep nasal notch. The forehead is low and steeply inclined with low frontal eminences (Line Drawing 2). The absolute length of the frontal bone, as

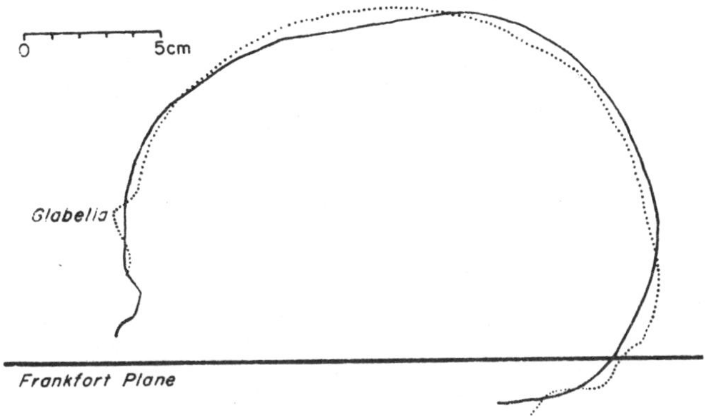

Comparative Craniograms of 1970-IV (solid line) and 1972-III (dotted line) specimens.

measured by chord and arc distances from Nasion to Bregma, is greater than the norms for the length of the frontal bone in anatomically modern *Homo sapiens*. The parietal bones have large eminences, a striking feature of most of the Sarai Nahar Rai skeletons of both sexes. The occipital bone, while severely crushed, has preserved its pattern of a uniform and even curvature of the nuchal region. Nuchal crests are low. The temporal bones support mastoid processes of moderate size and of pyramidical form. There are large external auditory meati. There is no indication of temporal fullness. Coronal and sagittal sutures are clearly visible, but their patency is rendered more obvious by postmortem erosion of the bones of the vault along articulating margins. The basi-occipital-sphenoidal suture has not fused. The face is hypereuryprosopic, and the nasal pattern is in the indicial category of low leptorhiny. The nasal profile is concave, and nasal sills are oxycraspedotic. Orbital form is chamaeconchic and rhomboid, and orbital margins are dull. The malars are robust but not large, and they project anteriorly rather than laterally. Upper and total facial prognathism is moderate, but alveolar prognathism is pronounced. The palate is deep and brachystaphaline. As with other crania of this series, the intraorbital breadth is greater than is encountered in most skulls of anatomically modern *Homo sapiens* from South Asia.

The mandible, while of moderately large size, is not especially robust. The mylohyoid crests are low, gonia are straight, and Pterygoid muscular impressions are low. The mental eminence is large and bilateral in form. Genial tubercles are paired and low. The croupus-ramus angle is steep as is most common in male specimens. The dentition is complete except for the postmortem loss of RIT. The third molars have erupted and are slightly worn; the $LM\bar{3}$ is worn to a somewhat greater degree than the $RM\bar{3}$ The pattern of wear is even across the occlusal surfaces of the teeth, but for the lower premolars the direction of wear is buccal. All anterior teeth show moderate wear, while posterior teeth have retained considerably more enamel on their occlusal surfaces. The cusp-groove patterns of lower second and third molars is + 4 and Y5 respectively. The wear on the first molars is too severe to allow for determination of these features. Hypocone variation and cusp number of maxillary molars is 4 for RLM1 , 3 fo RLM2, and +3 for RLM3 . Molar occlusal form is round. The order of molar size for the lower dentition is M1› M3› M›2; for the upper dentition this is M2› M1› M3. There is no evidence of caries, alveolar resorption is slight, and moderate enamel hypoplasia is evident on all upper and lower canines and incisors.

Of the postcranial bones, the vertebrae and ribs are large and indicative of a massive thoracic cage.However, the clavicle is not large or robust. Both acromial and sternal ends are completely fussed with the diaphysis. Completion of epihysial union of the acromial process commences at 18 years, and is completed by 21 years in males, providing a useful indicator of age at time of death for this specimen. The acromial end is rectangular in form. The scapula is a large bone, with prominent spine and robust axillary ,broder. Of the bones of the upper extremity, the proximal end of the humerus exhibits an epiphysial line; fusion of this part of the humerus terminates at around 21 years for males. The humeral diaphysis is straight and moderately robust, with a well marked bicipital groove. There is a trace of an epiphysial line on the proximal end of the redius; ossification of this portion is completed by the 18th year. The radial tuberosity is small, but highly elevated. The ulna shows complete ossification of the proximal end of the shaft. On the lateral aspect of the proximal end of the ulna is a deep and short groove, marking the attachment of Anconeus, as well as a large Supinator crest, which extends distally from the apex of the radial facet for some 30 mm. These features of hypermuscular development of the forearm indicate some habitual activity associated with brachial hyperextension, as in spear-throwing or use of a sling (Kennedy 1983). Unfortunately, the absence of a left ulna for this skeleton does not allow determination of its bilaterality, but, as will be noted in descriptions of other skeletons in this series, this unique occupational marker appears most oftern in the right ulnae of males.

The sex of this specimen is determined to be male on the basis of the high degree of muscularity of the cranial and postcranial bones, and the high frequency of male features in the mandible. Age at time of death appears to be within the range of 17 to 19 years, an estimate based upon dental evidence of eruption and wear of third molars, and the degree of suture closure and of epiphysial union of the long bones. No Pathologies are observed in this skeleton.

Skeleton 1973—IV

The poorly preserved cranial vault exhibits well marked nuchal crests, and a very large and robust external occipital protuberance. The mastoid process of the preserved right temporal bones has a pronounced supramastoid crest. Occipital bone thickness is 5 to 6 mm. The mandible, which is limited to the inferior margin of the right corpus, has gonium with some eversion and well-marked Pterygoid attachments. The mental eminence is missing, but the preserved corpus suggests that it was bilateral. Corpus length does not exceed 100 mm.

Of the bones of the axial skeleton, the sacrum is preserved as five unarticulated fragments. The curvature of the anterior surface of this bone takes its origin from the first sacral body. All vertebrae are present, and the lumbars and last three thoracics show pronounced arthritic lipping along the superior and inferior margins of their bodies, a condition which becomes most striking for the lumbar vertebrae 2 to 5 (Figure 15). The ribs have sharp crests and are fluted along their inferior margins. Clavicles are large with rectangular-shaped acromial ends. The scapulae are incomplete, but the glenoid cavities are preserved and are shallow and unlipped.

Figure 15. Osteoarthritic lipping of lumbar vertebrae of Skeleton 1973-IV.

Humeral diaphyses are large and straight. The right humerus has some normal cortical thickening at the proximal end of its diaphysis, a feature absent in the left humerus. Both humeri and radii have shafts which are straight and not particularly robust. The styloid process of the left ulna is large, but it is the right ulna which exhibits the greater degree of robusticity, particularly in the proximal area of the interosseous line and in the region of attachment of Anconeus and Supinator (Figure 17). The innominate bones are massive,

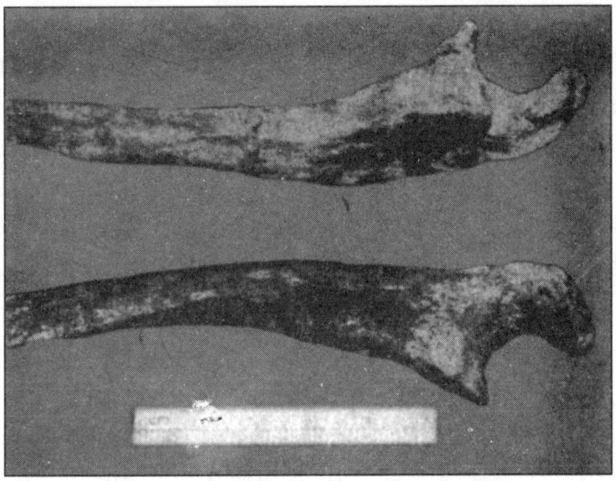

Figure 17. Hypertrophy of Supinator crest on ulna of Skeleton 1973-IV

with heavy and robust iliac crests, sharp arcuate lines, and large ischial tuberosities. The anterior iliac spines are well developed. Sciatic notches are deep and narrow, and there is no trace of a preauricular sulcus. Given these male features of the innominates, it is interesting that the Ischial-Pubic Index should fall between the male and female ranges. Of the lower extremities, the femora are straight and support large linea aspera with pronounced pilasters. The tibiae have large tuberosities, sharply defined and extensive Vastus lines, and large but single squatting facets. The fibulae are deeply fluted and exhibit considerable torsion. Foot bones are large. The right patella is larger than its left counterpart, and along its medial border are nodular excresences of secondary bone, which appear to be due to degenerative modifications, caused, perhaps, by arthritic inflammation of the joint of the right knee. The femoral morphology falls between the values for eurymeria and platymeria. The tibiae are mesocnemic.

On the basis of general skeletal robusticity, the sex of this specimen is defined as male. Only the Ischial-Pubic Index suggests femaleness, and this is due in part to the postmortem distortion and fracturing of the right innominate bone. Age at time of death is estimated as between 22 and 24 years, on the basis of modifications of the pubic symphysis. However, the drgree of lipping of the lumbar vertebrae suggests that this individual might be somewhat older. All bones show complete epiphysial union, but cranial sutures remained patent at time of death. The most obvious pathology observed is an arthritic condition of the lumbar vertebrae and the right patella.

Skeleton 1972-IX

There is no skull associated with this specimen. Of the bones of the thorax, the sternum is represented by a complete manubrium, with a sahllow jugular notch, and pronounced concavity of its anterior surface. The sacrum has six fused segments, and is of homobasal form. Anterior curvature of the sacrum is minimal, and is limited to the area of the first two sacral bodies. The thoracic vertebrae are severely damaged, but they do not appear to exhibit the pronounced degree o arthritic lipping which is present in the bodies of the lumbar vertebrae. The second lumbar vertebrae has considerable resorption of compact bone tissue, and the body is compressed. There is some porosity and striation on the corpus of this bone, which is suggestive of the degree of bone modification commonly seen in individuals in their late fourth decade of life or later. The first lumbar vertebra does not show any modification of a pathological nature. Ribs are large, and have sharp interosseous crests. The clavicles are fragmentary, but a preserved sternal end of a right clavicle indicates that the bone was large and robust. The fragment of right scapula is similarly distinctive for its muscular robusticity. The preserved right humerus shows a thickening of the proximal third of its straight diaphysis. The right ulna has some curvature of its proximal end, and its radial facet is 9 mm in length. The styloid process is large, and there is some arthritic lipping at the distal end. The radial tuberosity is very well developed on the right radius. The bones of the right hand are especially interesting, since the palmar surfaces of the proximal phalanges of digits 2, 3, and 4 show prominent tendinous development along their medial and lateral borders. This is less obvious on the proximal phalanx of digit 5. This degree of manual robusticity, not observed on the bones of the left hand, suggests the markings of an occupational stress where gripping and grasping functions were involved. The innominate bones and sacrum are embedded in a single piece of matrix, and only certain morphological features can be observed. However, it is possible to discern the illiac crest, which is broad and muscular, and the arcuate lines, which are dull. There is no sign of a preauricular sulcus on a fragment of one of the innominates. Bones of the lower extremity include femoral portions which indicate a massive and straight diaphysis, with a short but stout linea aspera mounted on a low pilaster. The transverse form of the femoral shaft is ovoid. Fovea of the caput is deep. The crista hypotrochanterica is pronounced, and is accompanied by a moderately deep fossa. The left femur is platymeric. The left tibia has a transverse form which is ellipsoid. The shaft is straight, retroversion of the head is moderate in degree, and the Vastus line is sharp. This tibia is leptocnemic. The left fibula is straight and moderately fluted. The patellae and bones of the feet are not present in the collection.

Although sex determination cannot be established from adequate observations of pelvic features, the high degree of muscularity of the other postcranial bones suggests that this specimen is male. He died between his 28th to 34th year, an estimate based upon the degree of ossification of all postcranial bones, and the advancing condition of arthritic modification of certain bones, especially in the lumbar vertebrae. No other pathological conditions were observed.

Skeletons 1972-X (Figure 13)

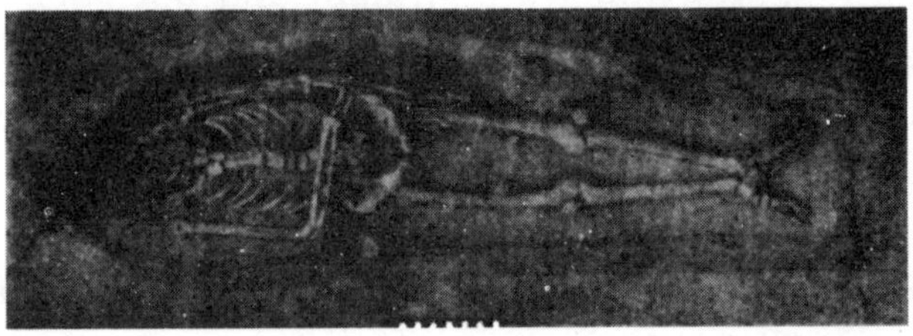

Figure 13. Skeleton 1972-X in situ.

The skull is preserved as seven large cranial fragments, some small pieces of maxilla, and a complete mandible with dentition. Examination of the bones of the cranial vault reveal a stout and rectangular-shaped left mastoid process, with a low supramastoid crest and deep digastric fossa, an elipsoid-shaped external auditory meatus, which is 16 mm in height, and an occipital bone of 7 mm thickness, with low nuchal crests.

The most striking feature of the mandible is its large size. Its ramus is broad and low. Gonia are moderately everted, and have large impressions for the Pterygoid attachments. The mental eminence is prominent, bilateral, and extensive. Genial tubercles are paired and low. The mylohyoid crests are very high. The internal surfaces of the coronoid processes are sharp. There is a considerable space between the distal surface of the RLM$\bar{3}$ and the ascending remus. All teeth of the lower dentition are preserved *in situ*. Some loose teeth ---RLPM2, RLM1, LM2 and LM3 ---represent the upper dentition. All teeth show extensive wear, with dentine exposed on all occlusal surfaces, thus obscuring the original cusp and groove patterns. The order of molar size is M1 > M2 > M3. Direction of wear is buccal for molars and premolars of the lower dentition. There is no evidence of caries, crowding, or malocclusion.

Of the thoracic bones, the sternum is represented by a well preserved manubrium which is robust and moderately concave on its anterior surface. The sacrum is long and narrow with five completely fused sacral segments. Its form is hyperbasal. Sacral formina are large. All vertebrae are preserved, and these show pronounced arthritic lipping of their bodies, especially for the cervicals and for the 4th and 5th lumbars. The bodies of these lumbar vertebrae are compressed. Interosseous crests are not particularly well defined on the ribs. Clavicles are robust with pronounced curvature, and their sternal ends are massive. This degree of muscularity is repeated in the scapulae, which have heavy axillary borders and deeply recessed dorsal surfaces. There is no evidence of a scapular notch or foramen along the superior scapular margin. The acromial process has the shape of a rectangle. Glenoid cavities are not lipped. The right humerus is more robust than the left humerus, especially in the area of the bicipital groove. There is perforation of the olecranon fossae of both humeri. The radii are straight with large tuberosities. There is a small exostosis at the distal end of the right radius, at a point just superior to the carpal facet. The ulnar diaphyses are straight save for some moderate retroversion at the proximal ends. The radial facets are large, and the styloid processes are long and massive. As in the case of Skeleton 1972-IX, the right hand exhibits robusticity of the palmar surfaces of the digits, which suggests a habitual grasping activity. This is not so apparent in the digits of the left hand, but both hands show advanced arthritic changes on the proximal and distal phalanges of the pollex, and on the medial phalanges of the other digits. This degree of bone modification would have been moderately incapacitating for an individual. There are no arthritic changes obvious on the carpal bones. The innominate bones are large, with thick iliac crests, sharp arcuate lines, and massive ischial tuberosities. The sciatic notches are deep and narrow. There is no preauricular sulcus on either innominate bone. The iliac spines are large and blunted. The Ischial-Pubic Index of 73.86 for the right innominate accords well with its estimation as a male pelvis on the basis of morphological observations. The left femur has a straight diaphysis with a high linea aspera and a pilaster which extends some 155 mm. The trochanters are not especially large, and the fossa of the hypotrochanteric region is shallow. The fovea of the femoral head is small and deep. The unusual femoral length of 512 mm is one of the striking features of this specimen. The femoral form is platymeric. The left tibia is also a large bone, with a massive tuberosity which extends some 49 mm along the straight shaft. There is no retroversion of the tibial head. There is a single elongated nutrient foramen. Squatting facets are of moderate size. The tibia is mesocnemic. The left fibula and both patellae are large, but without distnictive morphological features. The bones of the feet are well presrved. The right first metatarsal shows lipping at its proximal end, just inferior to the head, as well as along its plantar surface. This feature is less obvious on the other right metatarsals. The left first metatarsal shows the same kind of lipping, and, at the middle portion of its shaft, on the plantar surface, is a solitary osteocartilaginous exostosis (Figure 16). The apex of this bony

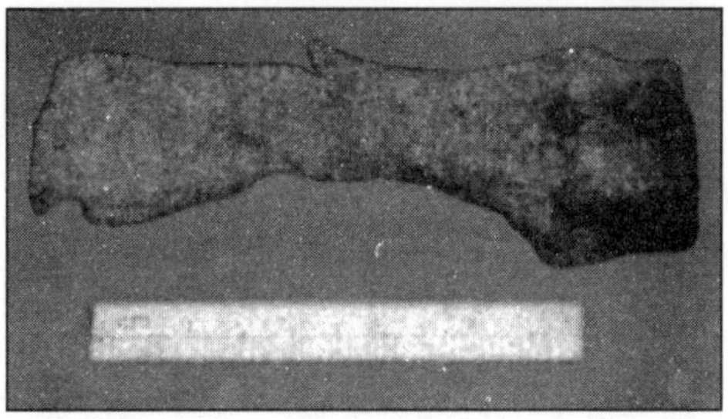

Figure 16. Exostosis on left first metatarsal of Skeleton 1972-X.

spine has been broken off postmortem.

Estimation of age based upon the data of the pubic symphysis is 22 to 28 years for this individual, with a mean age of 24.14 $\pm$ 1.93 years. This estimation agress with the dental evidence, as the RLM$\overline{3}$ have erupted and exhibit severe wear. Enamel is removed from the occlusal surfaces of the other molars as well. The extreme degree of muscular robusticity, and large size of almost all of the bones of this skeleton, indicate that its sex is male. The most striking morphological features of maleness are the steep angle of the mandibular corpus and ramus, the bilateral chin, the deep and narrow sciatic notch, the Gothic-arch form of the subpubic angle, the absence of a preauricular sulcus, and the value for the Ischial-Pubic indices. The existence of arthritic modifications suggests an early onset of degenerative changes in this individual. The solitary osteocartilaginous exostosis (or osteochondroma) is a form of benign tumor that is often the consequence of trauma. The massive tibial tuberosity and the long spinous process on the left first metatarsal are other unusual features of this specimen. Excavators of this specimen report that a stone projectile point was embedded in the left traverse process of the fifth lumbar vertebra (G. R. Sharma, personal communication). This object was photographed while the skeleton rested *in situ* (Figure 14), but the reported stone artifact was *not* observed by the present writers at the time of the laboratory study.

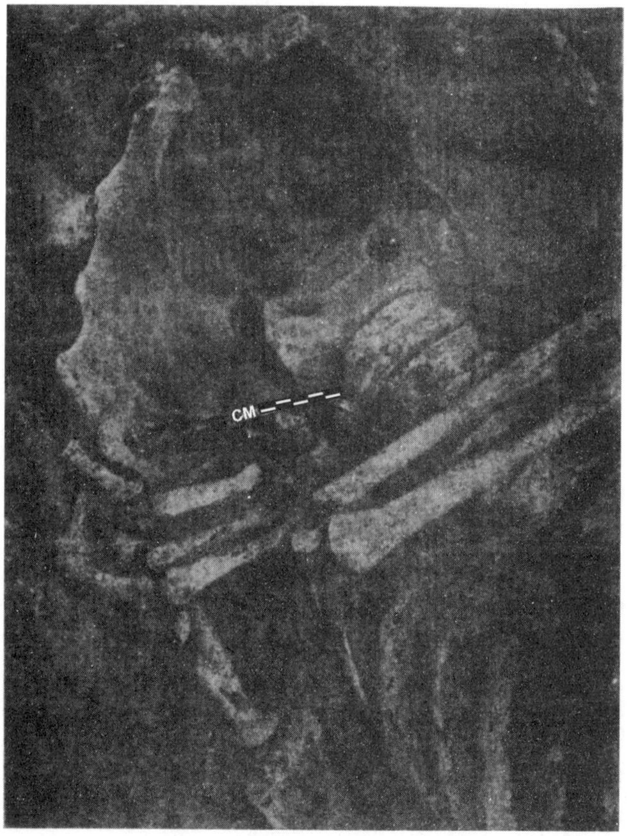

Figure 14. Details of Skeleton 1972-X, in situ. Note stone projectile point on left transverse process of the fifth lumbar vertebrae, above scale.

Skeleton 1973-III (Figures 11-12)

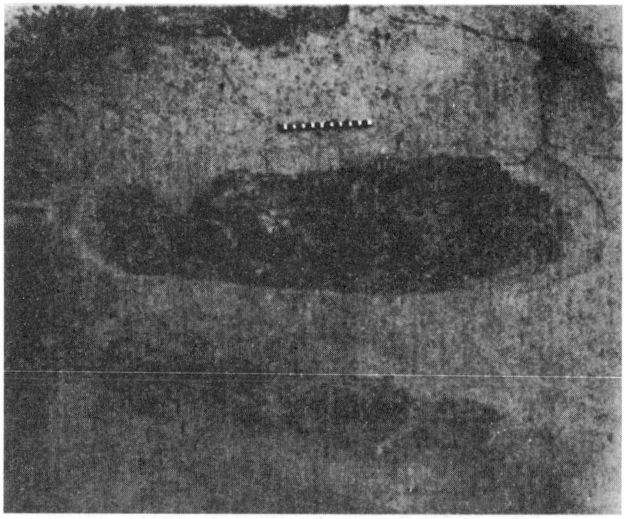

Figure 11. Skeletons 1972-II (lower), and 1973-III (upper), in situ.

Figure 12. Skull of Skeleton 1973-III in situ.

The cranial vault is well preserved, but it has suffered postmortem distortion due to pressure on the left side. There is flattening of the left side of the vault, and displacement of vault and facial bones towards the right side of skull. This is a large cranium. The frontal bone is not robust, and the supraorbital torus is low and median. Frontal eminences are pronounced in development, and the forehead is low with a vertical profile. The temporal lines are short and low. The parietal eminences are pronounced. The occipital bone has low nuchal crests, and the occipital profile is rounded. The mandibular fossae are deep and elongated. The temporal bones have large mastoid processes and moderately developed supramastoid crests. The external auditory meati are large and of oval form. All sutures remain clearly visible, the coronal suture being the most obviously patent. Facial bones show large and massive developements of the zygomae and maxilla. The orbital margins are dull. The canine fossae are low. There is a supraorbital foramen over the right orbit, but no foramen on the left side. The nasal profile is concave and the nasal sinus is broad. Nasal sills are orygmocraspedotic. There is some alveolar prognathism and total facial prognathism, but the upper portion of the face is not prognathic. The palate has a marked palatine torus. The face is very broad, but the degree of postmortem distortion precludes determination of the facial indices.

The partially preserved mandible shows prominently everted gonia, low impressions for the Pterygoid muscles, and an extensive but reduced mylohyoid ridge. There is a single low genial tubercle. Mental formaina are single on each side of the corpus. The chin is of bilateral form and moderately projecting. The angle of the corups and ramus is steep and suggestive of the condition found most frequently in males. The dentition is complete except for the LI$\bar{1}$ and LI$\bar{2}$ All third molars have erupted, however the lower set has not yet attained full eruption to the occlusal level of the the other mandibular molars. These third molars of both dentitions reveal no signs of wear, but other molars show slight wear, which is in a buccal direction. Premolars of the lower dentition show lingual wear to a greater degree. The most pronounced wear occurs on the anterior teeth, where dentine is exposed. Lingual pits and tubercles are on the upper lateral incisors, and all upper incisors show a shovel-shape pattern. Even the lower right lateral incisor has slight shovelling. The cusp and groove patterns of the lower molars are +5 for RLM3 +4 for the other molars. Hypocence variation f the RLM3 is 3, for the RLM2 is 3 and 3+ respectively, and for the RLM1 it is 4-. The occlusal form of the lower molars is square for RLM$\bar{1}$ and RLM$\bar{2}$ and oval for RLM$\bar{1}$

Of the bones of the axial skeleton, the sacrum is narrow with a low degree of anterior surface curvature along its course of five unfus segments. The sacral form is homobasal. All vertebrae are preserved, and are free of the arthritic lipping observed in other skeletons of the series. Ribs show moderate robusticity. Clavicles are large, with well formed acromial ends and prominent attachments for the Deltoid muscles. Axial borders of the scapulae are thick. The moderately robust humeri show recent completed ossification at their distal extremities. Epiphysial union is not complete on the radii. The degree of union cannot be determined on the ulnae. Metacarpal bones show advancing degrees of epiphysial fusion. The femoral head and diaphysis are in process of unification. The femora have a low degree of muscularity, an oval transverse pattern, and shallow foveae. The right femur shows high eurymeria. The tibiae are leptocnemic with low Vastus lines of elliptical transverse pattern. The left tibia is somewhat more robust than its right counterpart. Fibulae are incompletely fused at their diaphysial ends, and are only moderately fluted. Tarsal bones exhibit complete skeletal maturity.

The sex of this specimen is likely to be female on the basis of the gracility of all of the postcranial bones, and the specific female features of the skull, which include the large frontal and parietal bosses, low and median supraorbital torus, low nuchal crests and temporal lines, and the reduction in size of the mylohyoid ridges of the mandible. Age at time of death is estimated to be between the 17th and 20th year. Cranial sutures are patent, and many of the long bones have not completed their epiphysial union. However, the best determinant of age is the pelvic data, which yield a score of 3 for all components for females and give a range of 18 to 23 years with a mean age of 21.50 $\pm$ 3.10 years. This estimate, however, based upon methods proposed by Gilbert and McKern (1973) in their classification of aging changes of the pubic symphysis, seems a bit high when compared with the degree of epiphysial union of long bones. The distal epiphysis of the right ulna is united and this takes place most frequently between the 21st and 22nd year. There is incomplete ossification of the ilium and this is completed by 22 years. Epiphyseal lines appear on the humerus and suggest an age of 17 years, and the condition of the femoral head suggests an age closer to 18 to 19 years. The calcaneus has completed its growth, as it does after the 18th year. Thus the age range of 17 to 20 years seems most appropriate for this female specimen. Pathologies were not observed.

Skeleton 1972-V

At the time of its discovery, this skeleton was assumed to be a female of 23 to 24 years of age at time of death. Later it was estimated to have had a living stature of considerable height (Sharma *et al.* 1980). When the remains were collected, the skull was not included, and analysis is limited to rather poorly preserved postcranial bones. The sacrum is preserved as six large fragments, which are unsuitable for morphometric analysis. Of the vertebrae which were collected, the 4th lumbar vertebra exhibits pronounced arthritic lipping. Ribs are fragmentary. A right ulna shows completion of epiphysial union and moderate to well developed interosseous crests. These same features are recognized in the radial fragments. The phalanges of the right hand show considerable robusticity of their plantar surfaces, a feature not so pronounced in the bones of the left hand. Epiphysial union is complete for all hand bones. The innominate bones have broad and shallow sciatic notches, preauricular sulci, and complete ossification of the iliaccrests. The femora appear to have well developed pilasters, and the left femur has a prominent linea aspera. The collodiaphysial angle is intermediate between values common to males and females. Tibiae are fragmentary, and the fibulae adhere to them by a bond of hard calcareous cement. This specimen is probably a female as the bones are generally gracile, compared to male specimens of this population which are hyper-robust. The pattern of the sciatic notch is most certainly female. The only clues to age at time of death are the completion of epiphysial union and the pronounced arthritic lipping of the lumbar vertebra. This appears to be an individual who died in the first half of the fourth decade of life. No anomalies of the skeleton were observed.

Skeleton 1972-XIII

This specimen has been described as female, with a stature of 170 cm (Sharma 1973). There is a calvarium and maxilla which are preserved as separate and unarticulated portions of the cranium. There has been some lateral compression of the vault, so that the left side protrudes, and all sutures are open as a consequence of this degree of postmortem distortion. The bones of the vault are held in place by the endocranial matrix of hard earth. The frontal bone has a low and median supraorbital ridge, and is low to moderate in forehead elevation. The forehead is vertical in profile, and forms an even curve from Nasion to Bregma. There is no nasal notch. The temporal lines are sharp, but lose this pattern as they sweep posteriorly to the coronal suture. The superior orbital margin is sharp. Intraorbital breadth appears to be great, but damage to the specimen precludes a metrical assessment of this feature. Frontal eminences are low, but parietal eminences are very prominent. The occipital bone has an even curvature in the nuchal area, and is not surmounted by large nuchal crests. The superior nuchal crest is mound-shaped and low.

Temporal bones are large with short but stout mastoid processes, medial to which are deep digastric fossae. Their supramastoid crests are low. The external auditory meati are of moderate size and ovoid in form. Mandibular fossae are deep and extensive. This feature and the low temporal lines suggest that the mandible must have been of moderate size and of a low degree of muscularity. The fragments of right nasal bone preserved indicate a slight concavity of the nasal profile at the root of the nose. The maxilla shows moderate robusticity. The palate is as deep as 13 mm. Unification of the interpalatine suture is nearing completion.

All teeth of the upper dentition are present, although the crown is missing from RT2 . The RLM3 are fully erupted, with no visible signs of wear on the LM3 and a trace of wear on the RM3 Hypocone variation of the RLM3 is 4 and 3+ respectively, 4- for the LM2 and RM1 , and 4 for the RM2 and LM1 The wear pattern is lingual for the molars and premolars, with greatest wear occurring on the anterior dentition. There is no marginal resorption nor any evidence of dental pathology. The RLM1 have a square occlusal pattern while the other molars are oval. The order of molar size is M1 M2 M3.

Of the bones of the axial skeleton, the sacrum is too incomplete to merit analysis of its number of segments or degree of curvature. Thoracic and lumbar vertebrae are present, but they are damaged. Ribs are large, and have marked interosseous crests. The scapulae are of moderate size, and the glenoid cavity of the right scapula does not reveal any lipping along its margins. The humeri show that the proximal epiphyses are in process of fusion, and, along the epiphysial line, the demarcation is deep and well defined. The distal ends of the bones show more advanced degrees of closure. Muscularity is low, and the bicipital grooves are shallow on these bones. The radii show unification of the proximal ends, but the distal epiphysis of the right radius is preserved as a separate piece of bone. The radial shafts are straight, rather gracile, with small and stout Deltoid tuberosities. Ulnar epiphyses are unfused, and the proximal caps are preserved as separate bones. There is pronounced curvature of the proximal half of the diaphysis. Proximal ends of the proximal phalanges of the hand are ununited and preserved as separate pieces of bone. The right innominate bone is present, and restored from several fragments. Its iliac crest has not completed ossification. The sciatic notch is broad and shallow. There is a single and low preauricular sulcus. The arcuate line is sharp, especially along its extension along the pubic bone. Muscularity is not pronounced on the iliac crest or ischial tuberosity. Anterior and psoterior spines are sharp. The well presrved left femur is in process of epiphysial union, and has a low tuberoisty and slight degree of muscularity. The left fibula is deeply fluted, and the interosseous crests are high. The fibular shaft is straight. Foot bones and patellae are present, and their states of development accord with the growth patterns of the other postcraninal bones of this individual. The femur is eurymeric. The tibia is leptocnemic. The postcranial bones are large, but they are not especially robust, even granting the young skeletal age of this individual.

The sex of Skeleton 1972-XIII is assumed to be female on the basis of these observations, as well as upon the cranial evidence of gracility, form of the frontal bone, pronounced parietal bosses, low nuchal and temporal lines, and curvature of the occipital bone. The sciatic notch is very broad and characteristically female. The Ischial-Pubic Index of 83.00 is well within the range of modern white females. The pelvic evidence is equally convincing for age determination, as the score of O for all components suggests an age range of 14 to 18 years, with a mean age of 16 $\pm$ 2.82 years. Femoral age based upon epiphysial union suggests a period of life between 15 to 17 years. The age of beginning epiphysial union for the distal end of the femur is 17 to 18 years, and the latest age of incomplete epiphysial union is 20 years, therefore the age of the femur is closest to 17 years. However, for the greater trochanter, union begins at 14 to 15 years, being completed by 18 years. Hence the age of the femur on this criterion is closest to 15 years. Dental evidence indicates complete eruption of the third molars with minimal or no wear, suggesting a dental age of around 17 years or slightly earlier. Thus we have an estimated age, for this female specimen, of from 15 to 17 years. There were no observed pathologies associated with this skeleton.

Skeleton 1970-IV

The first published description of this specimen appeared in *Nature* on 15 October 1971, along with a photograph of the frontal aspect of the cranium (Dutta 1971). Subsequent references to the sepcimen appeared in publications authored by Dutta (1973, 1984) and his associates (Dutta et al. 1971; Dutta et al. 1972). The most detailed description of Skeleton 1972-IV appears in Dutta's paper of 1984. The morphometric analysis which follows is based upon the data presented in these sourees, as well as upon observations made by the senior and second authors at the time of their visit to the Anthropological Survey of India.

The cranium is complete, save for some postmortem damage to the basalar aspect. The vault is large and its form is mesocranic, chamaecranic, and tapeinocranic. Inspection from the right or left lateral aspects reveals extreme flattening of the vault. This condition is reflected as well in the Cranial Auricular Height-Length Index of 59.89. Dutta's (1984: 41) estimation of cranial capacity is 1449.20 cm^3, based upon the Lee-Pearson (1901:247) formula for males. This value exceeds, by 112.68 cm^3, the estimate obtained by the present writers using the same formula. Observed vertically, the vault is of brisoid form with its maximum breadth across the plane of the parietal eminences. The forehead is broad, very low, and slightly inclined, with frontal eminences of moderate development. Glabella is pronounced, and the supraorbital tori, while bilateral, build to their greatest degree in the glabellar region. Supraorbital notches are moderately developed. The occipital region is slightly protruding with well marked nuchal crests and a prominent union. There is considerable bregmatic and lambdoid depression (Line Drawing 2). The

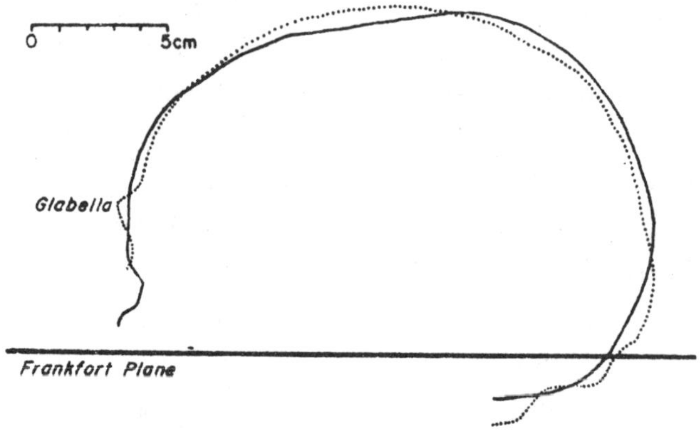

Comparative Craniograms of 1970-IV (solid line) and 1972-III (dotted line) Specimens

mastoid processes are long, heavily muscled, and surmounted by large supramastoid crests. The external auditory meati are of oval form. Pterion is of sphenoparietal type. All sutures of the cranial vault are open, and a single wormian bone appears on the left occipital suture at *pars asterica.* The face is hypereuryne, with chamaeconchic and rectangular orbits and a chamaerrhine nasal form. The orbits are set widely apart. The nasal bridge is low, and the root is slightly depressed adjacent to a moderately deep nasal notch. There is a moderate degree of upper facial prognathism and somewhat more pronounced alveolar prognathism. The canine fossae are shallow, but there is some furrowing of the subnasal portion of the maxilla. The palate is brachystaphaline and of moderate depth.

The maxillary permanent dentition is well preserved and complete. The RLM3 have fully erupted, the LM3 revealing no sign of wear. Dutta et al. (1972: 121) suggests that this tooth erupted later than the RM3 which shows slight wear, but another possibility is that one side of the mouth was receiving greater attritional-abrasional stress. This could be due to any one of a variety of reasons, unrelated to dietary functions. Dentine is visible on the anterior teeth, second premolars, and second molars, but first premolars and first molars show only moderate wear. The wear pattern of the central incisors suggests an edge-to-edge bite. Hypocone variation is of the 4 pattern for RLM1and 4- for RLM2and RLM3 Incisors are shovel-shaped to a very slight degree, and the RLI2have small lingual tubercles. The dentition is mesodont. There is no evidence of dental pathology.

All postcranial bones show robust features. The clavicles have well marked muscular impressions on their medial ends. The coronoid tubercle is well developed, but the attachment for Deltoid is not prominent. The subclavian groove is shallow. The right humerus has a prominent Deltoid tuberosity, and its bicipital groove is deep. Ulnar robusticity is exhibited by prominent Supinator ridges and interosseous crests. The right radius is larger and more developed than the left, but radial tuberosities are prominent on both bones. The Humerus-Radius Index is mesocercic. The innominates have deep and narrow sciatic nothces and large acetabular cavities. Muscular features of the iliac crest are prominent, and the subpubic angle appears to have been less than 90 degrees. The robust femora are eurymeric, the right femur being somewhat large than the left. The Humerus-Femur Index indicates a short femur relative to the upper arm. Patellae are broad. Tibiae have well marked Soleus lines and are mesocnemic. The left tibia is shorter than the right. The Tibia-Femur Index is brachycnemic. Squatting facets are present on the tibiae. Fibulae, while incomplete, have well deifined interosseous crests.

This is a male specimen, as demonstrated by the marked robusticity of cranial and postcraninal bones, blunt orbital margins, large mastoid processes, the form of the sciatic notch, and narrowness of the subpubic angle. The Ischial-Pubic Index falls within the values for males. The age of this specimens at time of death has been estimated as around 40 years by Dutta and his associates (Dutta et al. 1972: 117-118). Their aging criteria are a set of standards for dental wear proposed by Pal (1970, 1975) for *modern* Indian cranial remains. They dismissed suture closure as invalid for age determination, because another author (Brothwell 1963: 38) argued that this method had fallen into disfavour. They do note, however, tha the sutures of the vault remain patent. Quite correctly, they note the late timing of the ossification of the medial end of the clavicle, claiming that this takes place by age 30. However, Stevenson (1924) gives a mean age of 27 years for the latest age of incomplete epiphysial union of the clavicle, as determined by gross anatomical observation Furthermore, Stewart (1979) warns his readers to be aware of variation in the appearance of the sternal epiphysis of the clavicle towards the end of the third decade of life. The present authors suggest a younger age for this specimen, which they base upon the degree of cranial synostosis, absence of wear on the recently erupted LM3 minimal wear of RM3 and the degree of clavicular ossification. This new estimate would be an age range of 24 to 28 years for Skeleton 1970-IV.

PALAEODEMOGRAPHY

Sex and Age Distribution

The Sarai Nahar Rai skeletal series is composed of 15 specimens. Of the 10 described in this report, 7 are males and 3 are females. Children were not found at the site, although immature skeletons appear in the series from Mahadaha. The present sample is too small to suggest that Sarai Nahar Rai was predominantly a cemetery for males.

The extremes of the age range for males in the series is 16 to 34 years at time of death, with mean age ranges of 17 to 31 years. This has a cumulative mean of 23.28 years. This last figure is not statistically different from the cumulative-mean of 22.33 years for females whose extremes of age range are 15 to 35 years with mean age ranges of 16 to 32.5 years. There is no reason to believe one sex had a significantly greater lifespan than the other sex. It is interesting to note that these sex and age ranges for Sarai Nahar Rai do not coincide with the ranges obtained from the considerably larger skeletal series from Mahadaha. Of the 26 specimens descirbed from Mahadaha, 18 are identified as males, 6 as females, 1 is of uncertain sex, and there is a single child skeleton. The age range for Mahadaha males is 17 to 40 years, and form young adulthood to 60+ years for Mahadaha females. However, it appears that we are dealing with random samples for sex and age distributions at both sites, and the age range difference can probably be attributed to different sample sizes. Furthermore, the average ages at time of death for males and females at Sarai Nahar Rai agree well with death age means for Mesolithic populations elsewhere in India, in Sri Lanka and in Eurasia (Kenneedy 1984b).

Pathologies and Anomalies

With the exception of the osteocartilaginous exostoses (osteochondromae) observed on the right radius and left first metatarsal of Skeleton 1972-X (Figure 16), and the presence of dental

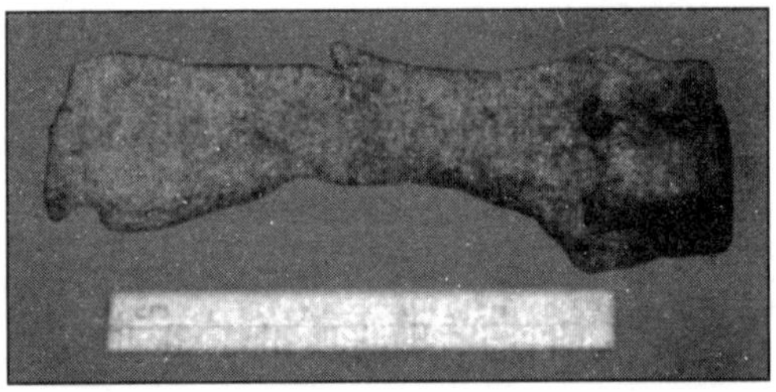

Figure 16. Exostosis on left first metatarsal of Skeleton 1972-X.

hypoplasia of the canine and incisor teeth of Skeleton 1972-III, other pathological features of the Sarai Nahar Rai series which were observed by the first and second authors are attributed to degenerative patterns of arthritic bone modification, or osteoarthritis (Table VII, Figure 15). What is most striking in this latter condition is the early age at which osteoarthritic changes are initiated in the Sarai Nahar Rai series, i.e., by the onset of

Figure 15. Osteoarthritic lipping of lumbar vertebrae of Skeleton 1973-IV.

the third decade of life. The apparent absence of dental pathologies, including caries, abscess, malocclusion, crowding, and high antemortem tooth loss, is another unusual feature of this Mesolithic collection, although other investigators (Lukacs 1981) have noted that, in Mesolithic series from India and Sri Lanka, a high frequency of severe dental wear is accompanied by a low incidence of caries and abscess. The single case of dental enamel hypoplasia among the Sarai Nahar Rai specimens may be attributed to any one of a wide variety of pathogenic agents, such as vitamin-D deficiency, exanthemateous fevers or hypoparathyroidism. Any of these or related pathological conditions may lead to interruption of dental development in the phase of active enamel formation. Dental enamel hypoplasia may be viewed as one stress marker of arrested ontogenetic development in the course of the attainment of full growth potential of the individual.

Some investigators, who had observed one or two of the Sarai Nahar Rai skeletons prior to the initiation of the present study, have suggested the presence of pathological conditions other than those just discussed. The investigators at the Anthropological Survey of India conclude that the flattening of the right frontal region of the skull, and the shortening of the limb bones on the left side of the body of Skeleton 1970-IV are diagnostic of a pathological condition defined as "left hemiperesis", i.e., this individual suffered from " a minor birth trauma leading to incomplete infantile hemiperesis. This condition-might also occur due to congenital aplasia or hypoplasia of (the) right side of the frontal cortex extending on to the right parietal region. This change is likely to affect the normal development of the left side of the body in general"(Dutta et al. 1972: 119-120,124). This is a most provocative speculation; however, a diagnosis of this order must be based upon accurate differentiation of bone shape modifications due to postmortem warping, from bone modeling which is the consequence of pathological malformation. It should also be noted that the differences in maximum lengths of long bones for the right and left sides of the body do not exceed 2 mm, nor do limbs of either side of the body exhibit marks of atrophy or neurological dysfunctions. Therefore, we do not concur with this diagnosis.

More recently, A. K. Sharma (1980) has described, under the rubrics of "palaeopathological observations" and "congenital perforation", the anomaly of olecranon fossa perforation of the humeri of Skeleton 1972-X. It is Sharma's understanding that "due to occupational hazards, work that requires constant vertical movement of the fore-arm, this thin bony membrane (in the olecranon fossa of the humerus) slowly gets rubbed, due to constant strokes of the olecranon of ulna, ultimately resulting in the creation of (a) perforation". If this explanation were correct, then the perforation is a marker of stress, and any "congenital" association it might have would be inherent in the capacity of some humeri to develop such perforations. The preforation *per se* is not a congenital or a pathological feature. However, the present authors do not see the matter in quite the same way that it is understood by Sharma, since it has never been demonstrated that the erratic frequencies in which this trait occurs in living primate populations (including orangutans and human beings from middle Europe, the Veddas of Sri Lanka, the Semang of Malaya, etc.) are related either to congenital determinants or to "occupational hazards". Current anthropological opinion is that perforation of the olecranon fossa is a marker of physiological stress, in a very broad sense, during the skeletal maturation of ontogenetic development, rather than a result of specific brachial activities of apes and men. We do agree with Sharma's analysis of the osteocartilaginous exostosis of the left first metatarsal of Skeletons 1972-X, which he ascribes to "some injury when the bony parts of the individual were still in process of growth". The extent of this bony spine is just under 9 mm in length (Table VII, Figure 16).

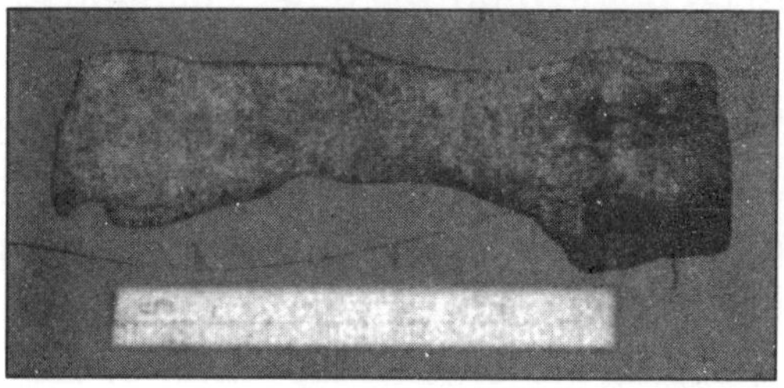

Figure 16. Exostosis on left first metatarsal of Skeleton 1972-X.

In the category of nonpathological anomalous features of the Sarai Nahar Rai skeletal series, we see three examples of squatting facets on the distal ends of male tibiae. More common, although not exclusively in males, is the hyperdevelopment of the attachments for the Anconeus and Supinator muscles in the region of the ulna, just inferior to the radial facet (Figure 17). When

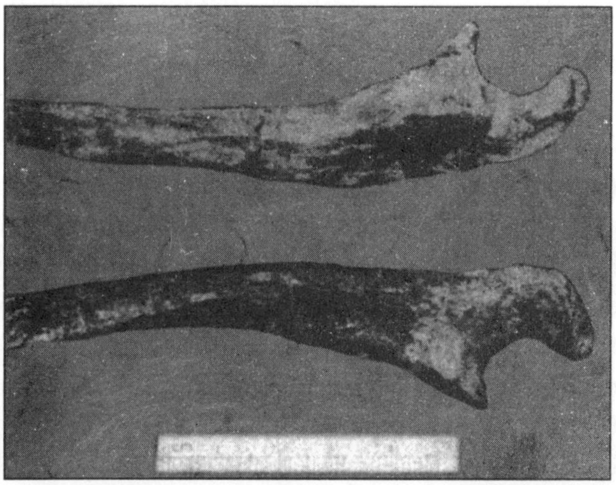

Figure 17. Hypertrophy of Supinator crest on ulna of Skeleton 1973-IV.

this stress marker is encountered, it is almost always more pronounced in the right ulna than in the left. Since the function of Anconeus is hyperextension of the forearm, while the function of the Supinator muscle is supination, it is reasonable to surmise that this feature is an occupational, or habitual, stress indicator having to do with rigorous brachial activities, such as throwing a spear, using a slingshot or hurling stones. This feature of the right ulna has been observed by the present authors in Mesolithic skeletal series from Mahadaha and Bhimbetka. It is interesting that the skeletons which have this ulnar feature do not exhibit the other common anatomical stress marker of the upper extremity--- the hyperdevelopment of the tendonous attachments along the palmar surfaces of the manual phalanges. This latter feature appears among both males and females, and indicates some habitual set of grasping movements especially of the right hand. Speculations concerning the precise nature of these occupational features are legion, but we seem to have here something more specific than a marker of righthandedness.

In short, the dental and osteological health status of the Mesolithic population from Sarai Nahar Rai appears to have been unusually good from examination of this limited series, an impression that the authors have formed for the Mahadaha skeletal series as well.

Nutritional Status and Ontogenetic Growth

There are two features of the Sarai Nahar Rai skeletal specimens which are especially pertinent in determining their levels of attainment of full ontogenetic growth potential. One feature is the striking paucity of stress markers on bones and teeth, which are diagnostic of episodes of inhibition of normal skeltal development in many other prehistoric mortuary series, especially those from post-Mesolithic cultural contexts. The economic shift, from the nomadic hunting—gathering lifeway to the subsistence strategies based upon agriculture and herding practices, by Neolithic and more advanced food-producing communities, demanded a biological price which is manifested in reduced skeletal growth and by the high incidence of other markers of growth stress. These latter features include lines of arrested growth in the proximal and distal extremities of long bones (Harris lines), dental enamel hypoplasia, and excessive bowing or curvature of long bones which may be attributed to rickets among other conditions of malnutrition. Dental pathologies such as caries and abscess become more frequent in early and contemporary food-producing populations. However, with the exception of Skeleton 1972-III, the Sarai Nahar Rai series does not exhibit these or other markers of arrested growth or inadequate nutritional resources. It must be emphasized that dental enamel hypoplasia is not always a direct consequence of periodic or chronic nutritional stress. The condition may reflect a wide range of abnormal health conditions suffered by an individual during the earlier period of life when enamel formation is taking place. However, all hazards t health have some bearing upon frequencies and qualities of food intake and upon the metabolic response of the individual to diet.

The second feature relating to ontogenetic development of Sarai Nahar Rai specimens has to do with their stature. All but one of the specimens described in this series have attained full skelet maturity. As noted above, stature estimation for a skeletal specimen is based upon tables of regression statistics involving data obtained from the direct measurement of maximum lengths of long bones of the upper and lower extremities. To be sure, there are difficulties inherent in this method since tables of stature estimates for the long bones of one population may not be appli able to stature estimates of another population, especially when the populations are genetically distant from one another. Furthermore, different investigators have favoured the use of different methods for estimation of living stature from maximum lengths of long bones, and comparisons of their stature tables may show some incompatibility of results. Also, we must keep in mind that all of these standards for stature estimation are based upon studies of individuals from modern populations where an individual's recored of body height when alive is correlated with the maximum lengths of his long bones after death. Consequently, when determining statures for members of an extinct population, the skeletal biologist is unable to establish precise standards which are specific for a prehistoric series. Rather, he has recourse only to estimations of stature which are alredy available and based upon data from relatively contemporary samples of individuals. Even when an investigator working with prehistoric human remains from India does make use of stature tables incorporating data for modern South Asians (Athawala 1964), these are of dubious value if applied to an extinct population such as Sarai Nahar Rai.

Admitting then that existing stature estimation tables have certain limitations when applied to prehistoric populations, they are, nevertheless, essential in providing the skeletal biologist with a *relative* picture of stature in the past. For this reason, the Trotter (1970) tables are consulted in the present study (Table VI). Earlier standards, proposed by Pearson (1899) as well as Dupertuis and Haddon (1951), have their uses, but the more recent Trotter study includes a large number of individuals, and her standards for males and females of European descent are more appropriate in connection with the Sarai Nahar Rai specimens, than are tables for persons of African or Far Eastern descent.

In their study of Skeleton 1970-IV, the investigatiors from the Anthropological Survey of India measured the skeleton *in situ* and obtained a length of 165 cm. They justified this procedure by noting that the skeleton "was lying in a normal extended position on its back, and, there, the crown-heel measurement taken by a steel tape may be considered as representing the true length of the skeleton ...... Even allowing some error on either side for the absence of superficial soft tissues and also for possible shrinkages.... due to the drying up of the joint cartilages, we may say that the individual had a medium stature" (Dutta et al. 1972: 119). However, they found that this *in situ* stature measurement was not compatible with the estimates obtained from the methods of Pearson, and Dupertuis and Haddon:

By equation of	*Equation in mm*	*Variation*
Pearson	1680.406	+30.406
Dupertuis and Haddon	1749.003	+90.033
Trotter and Gleser	1740.300	+90.300
Measured Skeletal length	1650.000	-------

The Trotter and Gleser (1952,1958) tables of 1952 and 1958, which were consulted in the present study, yield a stature estimate for Skeleton 1970-IV which is well above the ranges for medium height. Dutta and his colleagues did not indicate in their report which of the long bones were used in their estimations of stature for any of the three statistical procedures they cite. The stature estimates obtained by the present investigators, with reference to *all* long bones suitable for measurement of maximum length, afforded a considerable range of body heights, all within the category of tall stature:

Males	*Females*
173.93 - 192.08	174.89 - 187.68

However, if we take the femur as the best indicator of stature with respect to the Trotter (1970) tables, we obtain the following ranges:

Males	*Females*
175.65 - 183.26	(No femora measured)

While stature is only one criterion for ascertainment of an individual's growth potential, it is an important one. Although the sample is small, the Sarai Nahar Rai population appears to be composed of tall individuals, females as well as males, and in this respect they share a physical resemblance to the Upper Palaeolithic peoples of

Europe and western Asia during terminal Pleistocene times. To the same degree they share stature norms with the South Asian Mesolithic population from Mahadaha, but later Mesolithic peoples from Langhnaj, Bhimbetka, Bellanbandi Palassa and other sites in South Asia are characterized by somewhat shorter statures.

EVOLUTIONARY CONSIDERATIONS

The Mesolithic skeletal series from Sarai Nahar Rai represents a phenotypically distinctive population in South Asia. It is unlike other mortuary series hitherto discovered from this part of the world and submitted to morphometric analysis. Its unique place in the biological history of man in South Asia is especially significant in the light of its antiquity. Like their contemporaries in Europe, Africa and in other parts of Asia, the people of Sarai Nahar Rai were anatomically modern hominids, i.e, *Homo sapiens sapiens*. While bearing some physical resemblances to their sapient collaterals to the west of the Indus, the Sarai Nahar Rai population is characterized by a spectrum of phenotypic characteristics peculiar to itself.

With respect to cranial architecture, these ancient people of the Ganga valley have large and muscularly robust skulls, which range from low mesocrany to hyperdolichocrany. The cranial vaults are tapeinocranic, and, in the case of Skeleton 1970-IV, chamaecrany is present. Among the males, these long and moderately elevated vaults are surmounted by prominent supraorbital tori, moderately large to very large mastoid processes with prominent supramastoid crests, and sharp temporal lines. The development of the nuchal lines varies from slight to pronounced in development. Parietal eminences are very large for skulls to both sexes. The faces of both sexes are hypereuryprosopic and hypereuryne, with nasal forms ranging from low leptorrhiny to chamaerrhiny. Orbits are rectangular, chamaeconchic, and have dull margins. When the skulls are observed in *Norma lateralis*, the faces exhibit exceedingly low foreheads which are either slightly bulbous and vertical or inclined. Frontal bosses may be moderately developed. The nasal notches are deep, except in Skeleton 1972-XIII, and the profile of the nasal root is concave. Total facial prognathism is slight, but upper facial and alveolar prognathism is present to a pronounced degree in Skeleton 1973-III. The molars are robust, although their sizes vary. Canine fossae are shallow. Nasal sills are dull. The intraorbital distance is great for all specimens. Palates are deep and brachystaphaline. Mandibles are massive and have everted gonia on which Pterygoid muscular impressions are well marked. Some of these mandibles remind one of the *Homc erectus* mandibles from Ternifine in North Africa and of the Heidelberg mandible, although the Sarai Nahar Rai jaws have well formed mental eminences.

The dentitions are characterized by moderate to pronounced wear, especially along the occlusal surfaces of the anterior teeth, by apparent low incidence of the Y5 cusp and groove pattern for lower molars, and by the absence of caries, abscess, crowding, malocclusion, and other common dental abnormalities. The teeth are mesodont and megadont.

Postcranial bones are consistently massive and robust for males and females. Femora are eurymeric. Tibiae range from leptocnemia to mesocnemia. The single case of an articulated pelvic girdle, for Skeleton 1972-XIII, has an indicial value for the pelvic inlet which is platypellic. The Humerus-Radius Index for Skeleton 1970-IV is mesocercic. Living stature was tall for both males and females. The major pathological feature relates to osteoarthritic changes, but the overall health status of the population appears to have been good. However, there are no individuals in the sreies who survived beyond the fourth decade of life.

These morphometric data concerning the Sarai Nahar Rai series are relevant to two major considerations concerning the course of human biological evolution in South Asia. First, we recog nize here an ancient population which was extremely successful in its adaptation to the hunting and gathering way of life carried out in an ecological setting of abundant food resources. Only in this way may we explain the physical responses of this population towards a high realization of their ontogenetic growth potentials and the low incidence of diseases related to nutritional stress. This pattern of adaptive success, or fitness, is not unique in prehistoric cultures antedating the invention of agriculture and pastoralism, as demonstrated by the skeletal and archaeological records from southern Europe and western Asia in terminal Pleistocene times. It occurs, too, in some populations of more recent times, such as the natives of the northwest coast of North America. But for every one of these instances of high adaptability among hunting and gathering peoples, there are myriad cases where this economic strategy has failed, has persisted as a marginal form of existence, or has undergone rapid acculturation to neighboring food-producing communities.

The evidence for successful biological adaptation to Mesolithic economic patterns is documented in South Asia by the rich archaeological record. This record attests to the attainment of some fairly sophisticated lifeways and socioeconomic strategies, well before the initiation of more advanced food-producing technologies and the shift from a nomadic to a sedentary existence. Surely the exploitation of new ecological settings by Mesolithic peoples, which allowed them to occupy a wide range of natural habitats and to pioneer areas only sparsely settled by their Palaeolithic forebears, is a significant expression of their cultural and social adaptability. The recently discovered cave paintings from Bhimbetka, and from other Mesolithic sites in India, and the lithic record of an advanced technology, established upon the manufacture of small precision tools, are other indicators that Mesolithic peoples were developing a man-made environment conducive to an enhancement of biological success for their communities of wandering bands. The Mesolithic lifeway of South Asia is coming to be recognized as a phase of high culture within the constrictions of the hunting and gathering economy, in the same way that the cave artists of prehistoric Europe achieved their unique cultural attainments and their success in adapting to their ecological settings in local areas of abundant resources.

The second evolutionary consideration is our need to appreciate the nature of the biological affinities of the Sarai Nahar Rai population with other Mesolithic populations in India and beyond. Some effort in this direction has been made by Dutta (1973), who compares the cranium of Skeleton 1970-IV with seven specimens from the Mesolithic site of Langhnaj, a locality in northern Gujarat. Dutta notes that there are similarities between these two populations with respect to cranial length, the form of the forehead, pronounced supraorbital tori, alveolar prognathism, chamaerrhine nasal form, and a few other features, while differences are in cranial and facial sizes and shapes, orbital forms, dental dimensions, and stature estimations.

Today, biological anthropologists have available, for comparative analyses, a broad spectrum of sophisticated statistical measures. These may be directed toward determination of degrees of biological distances among Mesolithic specimens from South Asia. One recently reported multivariate study is a principal-components analysis of 117 prehistoric South Asian crania form 15 prehistoric archaeological sites in India, Pakistan and Sri Lanka, to which were added data of 23 crania from Upper Palaeolithic sites in Europe (Kennedy *et al.* 1984). Specimens from Sarai Nahar Rai were included in the South Asian sample. Results indicated that their clustering with cranial series from Mahadaha, Langhnaj, Bellanbandi Palassa, and the Upper Palaeolithic series from Europe, was due to morphometric similarities of facial architecture. The variables which effected clustering of these specimens from prehistoric hunting-gathering populations include external and interanl palatal breadths, bizygomatic breadth, intraorbital breadth, bifrontal breadth, and nasion-prosithion height. It was observed that these factors are different from those involved with clustering of post-Pleistocene food-producing populations of various degrees of technological development (Line Drawing 3).

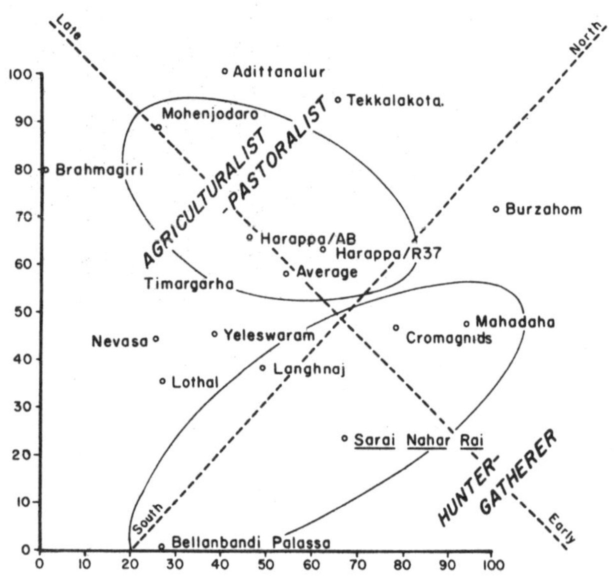

Axes and Clusters of Selected South Asian Prehistoric Crania Based upon Principal-Components Analysis.

Interpretation of these data does not rest upon an hypothesis of racial affinity whereby the prehistoric people of Sarai Nahar Rai could claim close kindred among European Upper Paleolithic people. Rather, it is proposed that the positions of the South Asian and European series reflect real differences in craniofacial anatomy which set apart prehistoric hunting-gathering populations from the more recent food-producing populations. These trends toward decreased cranial robusticity find their parallels in the shift from pronounced skeletal robusticity and large body size towards skeletal gracility and reduction of body size that has marked the course of hominid evolution over the course of the past 10,000 years (Wolpoff 1980). The evolutionary process behind this reduction of muscular-skeletal robusticity, with consequent reduction of sexual dimorphism, is natural selection, with smaller body size becoming adaptive for village and urban lifeways with their higher increments of carbohydrates and decreased availabilty of proteins. Another aspect of this trend is tooth size reduction which has been ably documented for prehistoric South Asians by Lukacs (1983,1984). Based upon observations made by Brace and Mahler (1971), it can be demonstrated that the smallest teeth appear among South Asian populations living today in the northern and northwestern portions of the subcontinent, while larger (megadont) dentitions survive in peninsular India and in Sri Lanka. The Sarai Nahar Rai dentitions show high mesodonty, a feature which was of adaptive value for pre-agricultural, pre-pastoral populations of South Asia. Thus, the Upper Palaeolithic European series used in this multivariate analysis finds its place near the series from Sarai Nahar Rai since it exhibits a parallel morphological dvelopment of facial size and cranial robusticity, and the large tooth size which is characterisitc of prehistoric populations of hunters and gatherers in widely separated regions.

The recovery of the human skeletal remains from Sarai Nahar Rai and from the nearby site of Mahadaha have brought Indian Palaeoanthropology into the arena of prehistoric hominid studies which have been associated for so many years with other parts of Asia and with Europe and Africa. The recent discoveries in Sri Lanka of fossil hominids dating to 16,000 years b.p., of which the published report will soon be available, will provide invaluable comparative material for further study of th Gangetic hominid fossil record. It is anticipated that the publication of our analysis of the Mahadaha skeletal series will also contribute to our understanding of Sarai Nahar Rai and firmly establish India in the context of advances made by human palaeontologists in other parts of the world.

ACKNOWLEDGMENTS

The laboratory analysis of the Sarai Nahar Rai skeletal series was undertaken by the senior and second authors in the autumn and early winter of 1980 in the Department of Ancient History, Culture and archaeology at Allahabad University, Allahabad, Uttar Pradesh, India. The senior author is deeply grateful to Dr. G. R. Sharma, Head of the department, for permission to examine the skeletal series as well as for the appointment of Visiting Fellow in the Centre of Advanced Study, Allahabad University. The single skeleton from Sarai Nahar Rai which is housed at the Anthropological Survey of India in Calcutta was made available through the courtesy of the urvey's Director, Dr. H. Rakshit. The assistance of Drs. A. Basu, P. C. Dutta, and A. Pal was indispensible to the completion of this facet of the project. The research program was sponsored by the National Science Foundation (Grant No. BNS 8014293) and the American Institute of Indian Studies (Smithsonian Award No. 00613900) during the senior author's year of sabbatical leave. Special thanks is expressed to Dr. John Yellen and to Dr. P. R. Mehendiratta, officers of these award foundations, and to Mrs. Margaret Carrick Fairlie Kennedy, whose assistance in the laboratory was invaluable. Dr. John R. Lukacs of the Department of Anthropology, University of Oregon provided valuable comments and suggestions in reviewing the manuscript prior to its publication.

REFERENCES

Agrawal, D. P., S. K. Gupta and S. Kusumgar, 1971a. Tata Institute Radiocarbon Date List VIII. *Radiocarbon* 13:84-93.

Agrawal, D. P., S. K. Gupta and S. Kusumgar, 1971b. Tata Institute Radiocarbon Date List IX. *Radiocarbon* 13:442-449.

Agrawal, D. P., R. V. Krishnamurthy and S. Kusumgar, 1985. Physical Research Laboratory Radiocarbon Date List V. *Radiocarbon* 27:95-110.

Agrawal, D. P. and S. Kusumgar, 1969. Tata Institute Radiocarbon Date List VI. *Radiocarbon* 11:188-193.

Agrawal, D. P. and S. Kusumgar, 1973. Tata Institute Radiocarbon Date List X. *Radiocarbon* 15:574-585.

Agrawal, D. P. and S. Kusumgar, 1975. Tata Institute Radiocarbon Date List XI. *Radiocarbon* 17:219-225.

Aitken, M. J., 1974. *Physics and Archaeology.* Oxford: Clarendon Press.

Allchin, B., 1958. Morhana Pahar: a rediscovery. *Man* 58:153-155.

Athawala, M. D., 1964. Estimation of height from lengths of forearm bones: a study of one hundred Maharashtrian male adults of ages between twenty-five and thirty years. *American Journal of Physical Anthropology* 21:105-112

Brace, C. L. and P. E. Mahler, 1971. Post-Pleistocene changes in the human dentition. *American Journal of Physical Anthropology* 34:191-203.

Brothwell, D. R., 1963. *Digging Up Bones.* London: British Museum of Natural History.

Carlleyle, A. C. L., 1883. Notes on lately discovered sepulchral mounds, cairns, caves, cave-paintings, and stone implements. *Proceedings of the Asiatic Society of Bengal* 1883:49.

-------, 1885. Report of tours in Gorakhpur and Ghazipur. *Report of the Archaeological Survey of India* 22:1-122.

Dassarma, D. C. and S. Biswas, 1976. Quaternary deposits of the Belan-Seoti valleys, Allahabad district, Uttar Pradesh. *Proceedings of the Fourth Indian Colloquium on Micropalaeontological Stratigraphy* 1976:33-39.

Deraniyagala, P. E. P., 1963. An open-air habitation site of *Homo spaiens balangodensis. Spolia Zeylanica* 30:87-110.

Deraniyagla, S. U., 1981. Prehistoric Sri Lanka: 1885-1980. In the *P. E. P. Deraniyagala Commemorative Volume,* P. L. Prematilleke, W. T. P. Gunawardana, and R. De Silva, eds. pp. 152-207. Colombo: Lake House Investments.

Dupertuis, C. W. and J. A. Haddon, 1951. Or the reconstruction of stature from long bones. *American Journal of Physical Anthropology* 9:15-53.

Dutta, P. C., 1971. Earliest Indian human remains found in a Late Stone Age site. *Nature* 233:500-501.

-------, 1973. The earliest skeletal remains of a Late Stone Age man from India. *Anthropologia* 11:3:249-253.

---------, 1984. Sarai Nahar Rai: the first and oldest human fossil record in South Asia. *Anthropologie* 22(1):35-50.

Dutta, P. C. and A. Pal, 1972. The earliest Indian human skeletal find and the estimation of stature. *Current Science* 9:334-335.

Dutta, P. C., A. Pal and J. N. Biswas, 1972. Late Stone Age human remains from Sarai Nahar Rai: the earliest skeletal evidence of man in India. *Bulletin of the Anthropological Survey of India* 21:1-2:114-138.

Dutta, P. C., A. Pal and B. C. Dutta, 1971. Sarai Nahar Rai: a Late Stone Age site in the plain of the Ganga. *Journal of the Indian Anthropological Sociey* 6:15-28.

Ehrhardt, S. and K. A. R. Kennedy, 1965. Excavations at Langhnaj: 1944-63. Part 3: The human remains. *Deccan College Building Centenary and Silver Jubilee Series* 27:1-73.

Foote, R. B., 1916. *The Foote Collection of*

Indian Prehistoric and Protohistoric Antiquities: Notes on Their Ages and Distribution. Madras: Madras Government Museum. 246 pp.

Gilbert, B. M. and T. W. McKern, 1973. A method of aging the female *os pubis*. *American Journal of Physical Anthropology* 38:31-38.

Gupta, S. P., 1972. *Disposal of the Dead and Physical Types in Ancient India.* New Delhi: Oriental Publishers.

Gupta, H. P., 1976. Holocene palynology from meander lake in the Ganga valley, district Pratapgarh, U. P. *Palaeobotanist* 25:109-119.

Hanna, R. E. and S. L. Washburn, 1953. The determination of sex of skeletons as illustrated by the Eskimo pelvis. *Human Biology* 132:21-27.

Hunter, E. H., 1935. Interim report on an excavation. Nagpur University Journal 1:28-57.

---------, 1936. Final report on the excavation in the Mahadeo hills. *Nagpur University Journal* 2:127-144.

Jacobson, Jr., 1979. Recent developments in South Asian prehistory and protohistory. *Annual Review of Anthropology*. pp. 467-502. B. Siegel *et al.*, eds. Palo Alto: Annual Reviews, Inc.

Karve-Corvinus, G. and K. A. R. Kennedy, 1964. Preliminary report on Langhnaj. *Bulletin of the Deccan College Research Institute* 24:44-57.

Kennedy, K. A. R., 1965. Human skeletal material from Ceylon, with an analysis of the island's prehistoric and contemporary populations. *Bulletin of the British Museum of Natural History* (Geology) 11:135-213.

--------, 1983. Morphological variation in ulnar supinator crests and fossae as identifying markers of occupational stress. *Journal of Forensic Sciences* 28(4):871-876.

------, 1984a. Biological adaptations and affinities of Mesolithic South Asians. In *The People of South Asia: the Biological Anthropology of India, Pakistan and Nepal,* J. R. Lukacs, ed. pp. 29-57. New York: Plenum Press.

---------, 1984b. Growth, nutrition, and pathology in changing paleodemographic settings in South Asia. In *Paleopathology at the Origins of Agriculture,* G. J. Armelagos and M. Cohen, eds. pp. 169-192. New York: Academic Press.

Kennedy, K. A. R. and P. C. Caldwell, 1984. South Asia prehistoric human skeletal remains and burial practices. In *The People of South Asia: the Biological Anthropology of India, Pakistan and Nepal,* J. R. Lukacs, ed. pp. 159-197. New York: Plenum Press.

Kennedy. K. A. R., J. Chiment, T. Disotell and D. Meyers, 1984. Principal-components analysis of prehistoric South Asian crania. *American Journal of Physical Anthropology* 64:105-118.

Kennedy. K. A. R., T. Disotell, W. Roertgen, J. Chiment and J. Sherry, 1985. Biological anthro—pology of Upper Pleistocene hominids from Sri Lanka: Batadomba lena and Beli lena caves. *Ancient Ceylon* 6.

Kennedy, K. A. R., V. N. Misra, J. R. Lukacs, C. B. Burrow and S. C. Tiwari. (MS) *The Human Skeletal Remains from Mesolithic Bhimbetka, India.* (in press).

Kennedy, K. A. R. and K. C. Malhotra, 1966. Human skeletal remains from Chalcolithic and Indo-Roman levels from Nevasa: an anthropometric and comparative analysis. *Deccan College Building Centennary and Silver Jubilee Series* 55:1-135.

Klein, J., J. C. Lerman, P. E. Damon and E. K. Ralph, 1982. Calibration of radiocarbon dates: tables based on the consensus data of the workshop on calibrating the radiocarbon time scale. *Radiocarbon* 24:103-150.

Lee, A. and K. Pearson, 1901. A first study of the correlation of the human skull. Philosophical Transactions of the Royal Society of London Series A 196:225-264.

Lukacs, J. R., 1981. Dental pathology and nutritional patterns of South Asian megalith-builders: the evidence from Iron Age Mahujhari. *Proceedings of the American Philosophical Society* 125.

Lukacs, J. R., 1983. Human dental remains from early Neolithic levels at Mehrgarh, Baluchistan. *Current Anthropology* 24:(3): 390-392.

-------, 1984. Dental anthropology of South Asian populations: a review. In *The People of South Asia: The Biological Anthropology of India, Pakistan, and Nepal,* J. R. Lukacs, ed. pp. 133-157. New York: Plenum Press.

Lukacs. J. R., V. N. Misra and K. A. R. Kennedy. 1982. *Bagor and Tilwarı: Late Mesolithic Cultures of Northwest India. Vol. 1: The Human Skeletal Remains.* Poona: *Bulletin of the Deccan College Research Institute.*

Martin, R. and K. Saller, 1957. *Lehrbuch für Anthropologie in Systematischer Darstellung mit besonderer Breuchichtingung des anthropologischme Methoden begrundet von Rudolf Martin* 1. Stuttgart: Fischer Verlag.

McKern. T. W. and T. D. Stewart? 1957. Skeletal age changes in young American males. Analysed from the standpoint of age identification. *Environmental Protection Research Division* (Quartermaster Research and Development Centre, U. S. Army, Natick, Massachusetts), Technical Report EP-45.

Michels, J. W., 1973. *Dating Methods in Archaeology.* New York: Seminar Press.

Misra, V. N., 1976. Ecological adaptations during the terminal Stone Age in western and central India. In *Ecological Backgrounds of South Asian Prehistory,* K. A. R. Kennedy and G. L. Possehl, eds. pp. 28-51. Ithaca, New York: Cornell University, Occasional Papers and Theses of the South Asia Program.

Misra, V. N., Y. Mathpal and M. Nagar, 1977. *Bhimbetka: Prehistoric Man and His Art in Central India.* Poona: Sakal. 26 pp.

Noone, N. A. and H. V. V. Noone, 1940. Stone implements of Bandarawela. *Ceylon Journal of Science* 3(1):1-24.

Oakley, K. P., 1964. *Frameworks for Dating Fossil Man.* Chicago: Aldine.

Pal, A., 1970. Patterns in dentine exposure in human molars. *Papers presented in Seminar on Physical Anthropology and Allied Disciplines.* Calcutta: Anthropological Survey of India.

---------, 1975. Patterns in dentine exposure in human molars. In *Bioanthropological Research in India,* H. K. Rakshit, ed. pp. 28-33. Calcutta: Anthropological Survey of India.

Pearson, K., 1899. Mathematical contributions to the theory of evolution: on the reconstruction of the stature of prehistoric races. *Philosophical Transactions of the Royal Society of London* 192A (1898): 169-244.

Rajagopalan, G., Vishnu-Mittre, B. Sekar, and T. K. Mandal, 1982. Birbal Sahni Institute Radiocarbon Measurements III. *Radiocarbon.* 24:45-53.

Ralph, E. K., 1971. Carbon-14 dating. In *Dating Techniques for the Archaeologist,* H. N. Michael and E. K. Ralph, eds. pp. 148. Cambridge, Mass.: The M.I.T. Press.

Sankalia, H. D. and I. Karve, 1949. Early primitive microlithic culture and people of Gujarat *American Anthropologist* 51:28-34.

Sharma, A. K., 1980. Some palaeo-pathological observations on skeletal remains from Mahadaha and Sarai Nahar Rai. In *Beginnings of Agriculture,* G. R. Sharma, V. D. Misra, D. Mandal, B. B. Misra and J. N. Pal, eds. Appendix 3. Studies in History, Culture and Archaeology 4. 237 pp. Allahabad: Abinash Prakashan.

Sharma, G. R., 1965. Comments. In *Indian Prehistory: 1964,* V. N. Misra and M. S. Mate, eds. pp. 76-79. Poona: Deccan College Research Institute.

-------, 1973. Mesolithic lake cultures in the Ganga valley, India. *Proceedings of the Prehistoric Society* 39:129-146.

------, 1975. Seasonal migrations and Mesolithic lake cultures of the Ganga valley. In *K. C. Chattopadhyaya Memorial Volume,* G. R. Sharma, ed. pp. 1-20. Allahabad: Dubey.

Sharma, G. R., V. D. Misra, D. Mandal, B. B. Misra and J. N. Pal, 1980. *Beginnings of Agriculture.* Studies in History, Culture and Archaeology 4.

Allahabad: Abinash Prakashan.

Stevenson, O. H., 1924. Age order of epiphysial union in man. *American Journal of Physical Anthropology* 7:53-93.

Stewart, T. D., 1979. *Essentials of Forensic Anthropology.* Springfield, Illinois: Charles C. Thomas.

Tite. M. S., 1972. *Methods of Physical Examination in Archaeology.* London: Seminar Press.

Trotter, M., 1970. Estimation of stature from intact long limb bones. In *Personal Identification in Mass Disasters,* T. D. Stewart, ed. Pp. 71-83. Washington, D. C.: National Museum of Natural History.

Trotter, M. and G. C. Gleser, 1952. Estimation of stature from long bones of American Whites and Negroes. *American Journal of Physical Anthropology* 10:463-514.

-------, 1958. A re-evaluation of stature based on measurements of stature taken during life and long bones after death. *American Jounral of Physical Anthropology* 16:79-123.

Wakankar, V. S., 1975. Bhimbetka: the Prehistoric Paradise. *Prachya Pratibha* 3:7-29.

Wolpoff, M. H., 1980. *Paleoanthropology.* New York: Alfred A. Knopf.

TABLE I. RADIOCARBON DATES FOR SOME INDIAN MESOLITHIC SITES

Site name	Radiocarbon dates	Reference	Comments
Bagor	12450^{+220}_{-210}	Agrawal *et al.* 1985	Unburned bone, inorganic
	5620 ± 125	Agrawal *et al.* 1971a	Unburned bone, inorganic
	5090 ± 85	Agrawal *et al.* 1971b	Unburned bone, inorganic
	4585 ± 105	Agrawal *et al.* 1971b	Unburned bone, inorganic
	3945 ± 90	Agrawal *et al.* 1971b	Unburned bone, inorganic
	6245 ± 200	Agrawal *et al.* 1971b	Unburned bone, inorganic
	6460 ± 180	Agrawal *et al.* 1985	Charcoal
	8090 ± 220	Agrawal *et al.* 1985	Charcoal
Langhnaj	3875 ± 105	Agrawal & Kusumgar 1969	"Contamination is probably high"; mixed bones from different skeletons and levels.
Lekhahia	3560 ± 105	Agrawal & Kusumgar 1969	Unburned bone, inorganic "Archaeological associations suggest these could be younger"
	4240 ± 110	Agrawal & Kusumgar 1969	
Mahadaha	4010 ± 120	Rajagopalan *et al.* 1982	Charred bone, inorganic
	2880 ± 250	Rajagopalan *et al.* 1982	Charred bone, inorganic
	3840 ± 130	Rajagopalan *et al.* 1982	Charred bone, inorganic
Mahagara	11550 ± 180	Rajagopalan *et al.* 1982	Shell, inorganic
	9830 ± 160	Rajagopalan *et al.* 1982	Shell, inorganic
	3330 ± 100	Rajagopalan *et al.* 1982	Charcoal
	10980 ± 190	Agrawal *et al.* 1985	Shell, inorganic
	13740^{+400}_{-380}	Agrawal *et al.* 1985	Shell, inorganic
Sarai Nahar Rai	10050 ± 110	Agrawal & Kusumgar 1973	Unburned bone, inorganic
	2860 ± 120	Agrawal & Kusumgar 1975	Charred bone inorganic

TABLE II. CONDITION OF PRESERVATION OF SKELETONS*

Specimen No.	1972-I	1973-II	1972-III	1973-IV	1972-IX	1972-X	1970-IV	1973-III	1973-V	1973-XIII
Sex	M	M	M	M	M	M	M	F	F	F
Skull										
Cranium	—	—	C	I	—	I	C	I	—	C
Mandible	—	I	C	I	—	C	—	I	—	—
Dentition	—	—	C	—	—	C	C	C	—	C
Thorax										
Sternum	—	I	—	—	I	I	F	—	—	—
Sacrum	F	F	—	I	C	C	F	C	F	I
Vertebrae	—	C	I	C	C	C	F	C	F	I
Ribs-R	F	F	F	F	F	F	F	F	F	I
Ribs-L	F	F	F	F	F	F	F	F	F	I
Pectoral Girdle										
Clavicle—R	—	I	—	C	F	C	C	C	—	—
Clavicle-L	—	C	C	I	F	C	F	C	—	—
Scapula-R	—	I	—	I	F	C	F	I	—	—
Scapula-L	F	F	C	I	—	I	F	F	—	I
Upper Extremity										
Humerus-R	—	C	—	C	I	C	C	C	—	C
Humerus-L	—	I	C	C	F	I	C	C	—	I
Radius-R	F	I	I	C	C	C	C	C	F	C
Radius-L	—	C	—	C	—	C	C	I	F	C
Ulna-R	F	I	I	C	C	C	C	C	I	C
Ulna-L	—	C	—	I	F	C	C	C	—	C
Manus-R	I	I	—	I	I	C	F	I	I	I
Manus-L	—	I	—	C	C	C	F	I	I	C
Pelvic Girdle										
Innominate-R	—	I	—	C	I	C	C	I	I	C
Innominate-L	F	I	—	I	I	C	C	I	I	C

Table II, continued

Specimen No.	1972-I	1973-II	1972-III	1973-IV	1972-IX	1972-X	1970-IV	1973-III	1973-V	1973-XIII
Sex	M	M	M	M	M	M	M	F	F	F
Lower Extremity										
Femur-R	F	I	—	C	F	—	C	I	F	C
Femur-L	F	—	—	C	C	C	C	I	F	—
Tibia-R	F	I	—	I	—	—	C	I	F	C
Tibia-L	F	I	—	C	I	C	I	I	F	—
Fibula-R	F	C	—	I	—	—	I	C	F	C
Fibula-L	F	I	—	C	I	C	I	I	F	C
Pes-R	—	I	—	I	—	C	I	I	—	I
Pes-L	—	I	—	I	—	C	C	I	—	C
Patella-R	—	C	I	C	—	C	C	—	—	C
Patella-L	—	C	I	C	—	C	C	—	—	C

*C = complete; I = incomplete; F = fragmentary; — = missing

TABLE III. CRANIAL MEASUREMENTS (mm) AND INDICES*

Specimen No.	1972-III	1970-IV	1973-III	1972-XIII
Sex	M	M	F	F
Cranium:				
Gleabella-Opistocranion length (1)	198	192		
Bieuryonic breadth (8)	135	146		
Basion-Bregma height (17)	153	124		
Bifrontotemporale breadth (9)	97	107	100	104
Bizygomatic breadth (45)		145		
Nasion-Prosthion height (48)	68	62.5		
Prosthion-Subnasale height (48-1)	19		19	
Nasal height (55)	48	48.5		
Nasal breadth (54)	23	26		
Orbital height - R (52)	31	30.5		
Orbital height - L (52)		31		
Orbital breadth - R (51)	39	40		
Orbital breadth - L (51)		41.5		
Interorbital breadth (50)	24	29.5		
Biorbital breadth (44)		113		
External Palate breadth (61)	58		64	
Internal Palate breadth (63)	37	44.5	38	
Internal Palate length (62)	54		62	
Palate depth (64)	13	14	13	
Molar Row length - R			30.5	31
Molar Row length - L			29	30
Premolar-Molar Row - R			43	45
Premolar-Molar Row - L			42	45
Nasion-Bregma chord (29-1)	123	116		115
Nasion-Bregma arc (25)	134	137		103
Bregma-Lambda chord (30)	137	117		133
Bregma-Lambda arc (27)	145	137		105.5
Cranial Capacity (Lee-Pearson 1901)		1449.20 cm^3 1336.52 cm^3		1515.65 cm^3

Table III. continued

Specimen No.	1972-III	1970-IV	1973-III	1972-XIII
Sex	M	M	F	F
Mandible:				
Condylo-Symphyseal length (68)	122	114		96
Bigonial breadth (66)	90	118		
Bicondylar breadth (65)	112			
Corpus length - R (68-1)		86		89
Corpus length - L (69-1)	89	86		88
Corpus height at M_2 - R	29.5	37		29
Corpus height at M_2 - L	29.5	33		29
Corpus thickness at M_2 - R	17	20		19
Corpus thickness at M_2 - L	16	22.0		18
Ramus height - R (70)	59			54
Ramus height - L (70)	60	67		
Minimum Ramus breadth - R (71)		45		40
Minimum Ramus breadth - L (71)	34	44.5		
Maximum Ramus breadth - R (71-1)				50
Maximum Ramus breadth - L (71-1)	44	54.5		
Bimental breadth (67)	48.5	55		51
Molar Row length - R	31	32		
Molar Row length - L	32	34		
Premolar-Molar Row - R	44	48.5		
Premolar-Molar Row - L	44	47		
Symphyseal thickness	10	19		16
Corpus-Ramus angle - degrees (79)	125	115		115
Symphyseal height (69)	34	38.5		31
Cranial length-breadth index	68.18		76.04	
Cranial height-breadth index	88.23		84.93	
Cranial height-length index	77.27		64.58	
Upper Facial index			43.10	
Orbital index - R	79.48		76.25	
Orbital index - L			74.70	
Nasal index	47.91		53.61	
Internal Palate index	68.51		89.00	61.29
Zygo-Frontal index			73.79	

*R = right side; L = left side; A-p = anterior-posterior; Lat. = lateral; I-S = inferior-superior. Measurements for skeleton 1970-IV are taken from Dutta (1984); numbers in parentheses refer to Martin and Seller (1957) code.

TABLE IV. DENTAL MEASUREMENTS (mm) AND INDICES*

Measurements (millimeters)	MD	BL	MD/BL	BL/MD	MD X BL	(MD + BL)/2
1972-III						
Maxilla						
RM3	8.7	9.6	90.63	110.34	83.52	9.15
RM2	10.1	10.0	101.00	99.01	101.00	10.05
RM1	9.8	9.8	100.00	100.00	96.04	9.80
RPM2	5.9	9.0	65.56	152.54	53.10	7.45
RPM1	6.0	9.2	62.22	153.33	55.20	7.60
RC	7.5					
R12	7.0					
R11	8.4					
LM3	8.1	9.4	86.12	116.04	76.14	8.75
LM2	9.8	10.1	97.03	103.06	98.98	9.95
LM1	10.4	10.3	100.97	99.03	107.12	10.35
LPM2	5.9	8.8	67.05	149.15	51.92	7.35
LPM1	6.4	8.7	94.12	134.39	55.04	7.50
LC	7.6					
L12	7.2					
L11	8.8					
Mandible						
RM3	10.0	9.2	108.70	92.00	92.00	9.60
RM2	9.8	9.0	108.89	91.83	88.20	9.40
RM1	10.3	10.0	103.00	97.08	103.00	10.15
RPM2	6.4	7.4	86.49	115.62	47.36	6.90
RPM1	6.6	5.8	113.79	87.87	38.28	6.20
RC	7.0					
R12	6.5					
R11	5.5					
LM3	10.5	9.5	110.53	90.47	99.75	10.00
LM2	10.0	9.1	109.89	91.00	91.00	9.55
LM1	10.3	10.0	103.00	97.08	103.00	10.15
LPM2	6.5	7.3	89.04	112.30	47.45	6.90
LPM1	6.8	5.8	117.24	85.29	39.44	6.30
LC	7.2					
L12	5.5					
L11						

Table IV, continued

Measurements (millimeters)	MD	BL	MD/BL	BL/MD	MD X BL	(MD+BL)/2
1973-III						
Maxilla						
RM3	8.8	9.4	93.62	82.72	9.10	
RM2	9.0	10.0	95.71	116.66	94.50	9.75
RM1	11.0	11.0	100.00	100.00	121.00	11.00
RPM2	6.5	8.4	77.38	129.23	54.60	7.45
RPM1	7.3	8.2	89.02	112.32	59.86	7.75
RC	8.1					
R12	7.9					
R11						
LM3	8.9	9.4	95.68	105.61	83.66	9.15
LM2	9.0	10.0	90.00	111.10	90.00	9.50
LM1	11.6	11.0	105.45	94.82	127.60	11.30
LPM2	6.1	8.1	75.31	132.78	49.41	7.10
LPM1	7.3	8.7	83.91	119.17	63.51	8.00
LC	8.3					
L12	6.9					
L11	7.9					
Mandible						
RM3	11.9	9.5	125.26	79.83	113.05	10.70
RM2	10.5	10.1	103.96	96.19	106.05	10.30
RM1	11.4	10.2	111.76	89.47	116.28	10.80
RPM2	6.4	7.5	85.33	117.18	48.00	6.95
RPM1	6.9	6.8	101.47	98.55	46.92	6.85
RC	6.5					
R12	5.8					
R11	5.1					
LM3	11.3	9.4	120.21	83.18	106.22	10.35
LM2	10.1	9.9	102.02	98.01	99.99	10.00
LM1	11.3	10.5	107.62	92.92	118.65	10.09
LPM2	6.5	7.0	92.86	107.69	45.50	6.75
LPM1	7.3	6.5	112.31	89.04	47.45	6.90
LC	7.0					
L12						
L11						

Table IV, continued

Measurements (millimeters)	MD	BL	MD/BL	BL/MD	MD X BL	(MD+BL)/2
1972-XIII						
Maxilla						
RM3	8.5	11.0	77.27	129.41	93.50	9.75
RM2	9.0	10.1	89.11	112.22	90.90	9.55
RM1	10.5	10.4	100.96	99.04	109.20	10.45
RPM2	7.2	8.8	81.82	122.22	63.36	8.00
RPM1	6.8	8.7	78.16	127.94	59.16	7.75
RC	7.8					
R12						
R11	9.0					
LM3	7.7	11.3	68.14	146.75	87.01	9.50
LM2	8.7	10.0	87.00	114.94	87.00	9.35
LM1	9.9	10.3	96.12	104.04	101.97	10.10
LPM2	7.2	9.2	78.26	127.77	66.24	8.20
LPM1	7.3	9.0	81.11	123.28	65.70	8.15
LC	7.2					
L12	6.5					
L11	9.0					
1970-IV						
Maxilla						
RM3	7.9	10.2	77.45	129.11	80.58	9.05
RM2	9.5	11.5	82.61	121.05	109.25	10.50
RM1	10.0	11.1	90.09	111.00	111.00	10.55
RPM2	6.6	10.0	66.00	151.52	66.00	8.30
RPM1	6.5	9.6	67.71	147.69	62.40	8.05
RC	8.0	9.3	86.02	116.25	74.40	8.65
R12	7.0	7.0	100.00	100.00	49.00	7.00
R11	8.7	8.5	102.35	97.70	73.95	8.60
LM3	8.0	10.4	76.92	130.00	83.20	9.20
LM2	9.2	11.5	80.00	125.00	105.80	10.35
LM1	10.2	11.2	91.07	109.80	114.24	10.70
LPM2	6.6	10.1	65.35	153.03	66.66	8.35
LPM1	7.0	10.0	70.00	142.86	70.00	8.50
LC	8.0	9.2	86.96	115.00	73.60	8.60
L12	7.0	7.0	100.00	100.00	49.00	7.00
L11	8.5	8.2	103.66	96.47	69.70	8.35

*MD = mesio-distal diameter; BL = bucco-lingual diameter; MD/BL and BL/MD = crown index; MD X BL = robustness or crown area index; MD + BL/2 = crown module; R = right; L = left.

TABLE V. POSTCRANIAL MEASUREMENTS (mm) AND INDICES

Specimen No.	1972-II	1973-II	1972-III	1973-IV	1972-IX	1972-X	1973-III	1972-XIII	1970-IV
Sex	M	M	M	M	M	M	F	F	M
Thorax									
Sternum:									
Manubrium height (2)					40	47			
Manubrium breadth (4)					53.5	57			
Manubrium height-breath index					74.76	82.45			
Sacrum:									
Anterior height (2)					104	115	112		
Anterior breadth (5)					115	108	94.5		
Sacral height-breadth index					90.43	106.48	118.51		
Vertebrae:									
Vertical ventral height T 9 (1)				21					
T 10				26		21			
T 11	19.5					20			
T 12						23			
L 1	23				24	22			
L 2				26	25				
L 3	24.5			24.5	26.5		21		
L 4				24	26	26			
L 5	28			24	24	24	22		

Table V, continued

Specimen No.	1972-II	1973-II	1972-III	1973-IV	1972-IX	1972-X	1973-III	1972-XIII	1970-IV
Sex	M	M	M	M	M	M	F	F	M
Pectoral Girdle									
Clavicle:									
Maximum length - R (1)						131			149
Maximum length - L		156	138.5	158		134	143		152
Mid-shaft diameter A-P-R (5)		15		14		15	14		
Mid-shaft diameter A-P-L		13	12	13		15	14		
Mid-shaft diameter I-S-R (4)		14		13		14	10		
Mid-shaft diameter I-S-L		11	9	12		13	9		
Mid-shaft circumference - R (6)		44		45 0		45.5	41		40
Mid-shaft circumference - L		38	38	44		45	38		40
Clavicle - Humeral Index - R						35.98			45.43
Clavicle - Humeral Index - L									
Scapula :									
Maximum length - R (2)									
Maximum length - L (2)			153						
Breadth - R (1)						109			
Breadth - L (1)			122						
Acromial Process length - R (10)									
Acromial Process length - L (10)				51		52			
Glenoid Cavity height - R (12)				38.5		42	43	38	
Glenoid Cavity height - L (12)			33	36		44		37	
Length-Breadth index			79.73						

Table V, continued

Specimen No.	1972-II	1973-II	1972-III	1973-IV	1972-IX	1972-X	1973-III	1972-XIII	1970-IV
Sex	M	M	M	M	M	M	F	F	M
Upper Extremities									
Humerus:									
Maximum length - R (1)				363		364	348	358	328
Maximum length - L (1)		357	336	361					
Head diameter A-P-R (9)				47		41		40	46.5
Head diameter A-P-L (9)			42	46		39			
Mid-shaft diameter A-P-R (6c)		22		23	22.5	22.5	22	19.5	
Mid-shaft diameter A-P-L (6c)		23	19	23		22	21	15	
Mid-shaft diameter Lat - R (6b)		26		25	18	23	21	20	
Mid-shaft diameter Lat - L (6b)		20	20	24		22	20	19	
Mid-shaft circumference - R (7a)		74		78	67	76	70	64.5	
Mid-shaft circumference - L		68	62	76		71	63	60	
Mid-shaft index - R		84.61		92.00	125.00	97.82	104.75	97.50	
Mid-shaft index - L		115.00	95.00	95.83		100.00	105.00	78.94	
Robusticity Index - R				21.48		20.87	20.11	18.01	
Robusticity Index - L				21.05					
Middle Index - R		118.18		100.68	80.00	102.22	94.45	102.56	
Middle Index - L		86.95	105.26	104.34		100.00	95.23	126.66	
Humero-Femoral Index - R									
Humero-Femoral Index - L				72.34					

Table V, continued

Specimen No.	1972-II	1973-II	1972-III	1973-IV	1972-IX	1972-X	1973-III	1972-XIII	1970-IV
Sex	M	M	M	M	M	M	F	F	M
Radius:									
Maximum length - R (1)				295	265	288	285		268
Maximum length - L		295				278			266
Head diameter Lat - R (4-1)		24	22	24	23	23	23		
Head diameter Lat - L		24		23		23	22		
Mid-shaft diameter A-P-R (5)		13		14	12	12.5	12	13	
Mid-shaft diameter A-P-L		13		13		13.5	12	14	
Mid-shaft diameter Lat - R (4)		15		18	15	15.5	16	11	17
Mid-shaft diameter Lat - L		16		15	16	15	11		17
Mid-shaft circumference - R		46		48	45.5	47	45	39	
Mid-shaft circumference - L		48		45		49	46	41	
Mid-shaft index - R		86.66		77.77	80.00	80.64	75.00	118.18	
Mid-shaft index - L		81.25		86.66		84.37	80.00	127.27	
Humeral-Radial Index - R									77.13
Humeral-Radial Index - L		82.63		81.26		79.12	82.75		
Middle Index - R		115.38		128.57	125.00	124.00	133.33	84.61	
Middle Index - L		123.07		115.38		118.51	125.00	78.57	

Table V, continued

Specimen No.	1973-II	1972-III	1973-IV	1972-IX	1972-X	1973-III	1972-V	1972-XIII	1970-IV
Sex	M	M	M	M	M	M	F	F	M
Ulna:									
Maximum length - R (1)			319	295	308	300			288
Maximum length - L (1)	312		316		307	295			
Semi-lunar notch height - R (8)	36	29	38	33	32	36			
Semi-lunar notch height - L (8)	36		38		33				
Mid-shaft diameter A-P-R (11)	14		17	13	17.5	15	17.5	12	
Mid-shaft diameter A-P-L (11)	13		17		18	19		13	
Mid-shaft diameter Lat - R (12)	17		14	14.5	13.5	12	14.5	15	
Mid-shaft diameter Lat - L (12)	14		12		14	12		15	
Mid-shaft circumference - R	52		52	58	52	45	53	45	
Mid-shaft circumference - L	47		53		50	42		46	
Mid-shaft index - R	82.35		121.42	89.65	129.62	125.00	120.68	80.00	
Mid-shaft index - L	92.85		141.66		128.57	158.33		86.00	
Middle Index - R	121.42		82.35	111.53	77.14	80.00	82.85	125.00	
Middle Index - L	107.69		70.58		77.77	63.15		115.38	

Table V, continued

Specimen No.	1973-II	1973-IV	1972-IX	1972-X	1973-III	1972-XIII	1970-IV
Sex	M	M	M	M	F	F	M
Pelvic Girdle							
Innominate:							
Maximum height - R (1)		222		223	131	203	210
Maximum height - L (1)				223	206	204	220
Breadth - R (6a)				155	210	126	138.0
Breadth - L (6a)	141	149		149		133	138.0
Acetabulum diameter I-S- R (22)		58		59	47	45	57.0
Acetabulum diameter I-S- L (22)			46.5	60		45	57.0
Sciatic Notch breadth - R (8)	50.5	38		42.5			
Sciatic Notch breadth - L (8)	51			42		41	
Pelvic Inlet diameter A-P (23)						97	
Pelvic Inlet diameter Lat (24)						120	
Innominate length-breadth index - R						62.06	65.71
Innominate length-breadth index - L						65.19	62.72
Pelvic Inlet index						80.83	
Lower Extremities							
Femur:							
Maximum length - R (1)							464
Maximum length - L (1)		499	480	512			462
Head diameter A-P- R (19)		49			47		45
Head diameter A-P- L (19)		49	44	46			45

Table V, continued

Specimen No.	1973-II	1973-IV	1972-IX	1972-X	1973-III	1972-XIII	1970-IV
Sex	M	M	M	M	F	F	M
Femur, continued							
Subtrochanteric dia. A-P - R (10)	26	29			32		
Subtrochanteric dia. AD-P - L (10)		28			32		
Subtrochanteric dia. Lat - R (9)	32	33			29.5		
Subtrochanteric dia. Lat - L (9)		34	32	34	29		
Mid-shaft diameter A-P - R (6)	34	34			29		33
Mid-shaft diameter A-P - L (6)		34	27	38	29	30	34
Mid-shaft diameter Lat - R (7)	29.5	28			24		26
Mid-shaft diameter Lat - L (7)		28	28.5	27.5	25	25	26
Mid-shaft circumference - R	101	97			87		
Mid-shaft circumference - L		97	90	103	86	87	
Bicondylar Breadth - R (21)							
Bicondylar Breadth - L (21)				80.5			71.5
Pilastric index - R							125.92
Pilastric index - L							130.77
Platymeric index - R	81.25	87.87					89.65
Platymeric index - L		82.35	90.62	76.47	108.47		89.65
Robusticity Index - R					110.34		12.88
Robusticity Index - L		12.50	11.70	12.94			13.11
Middle Index - R	86.76	82.35			82.75		78.78
Middle Index - L		82.35	105.55	72.36	86.20		76.47

Table V, continued

Specimen No.	1973-II	1973-IV	1972-IX	1972-X	1973-III	1972-XIII	1970-IV
Sex	M	M	M	M	F	F	M
Tibia:							
Maximum length - R (1)							391
Maximum length - L (1)		434		445		435	390.5
Mid-shaft diameter A-P - R (8)	29.5				29		38.5
Mid-shaft diameter A-P - L (8)	30	32	27	37	32	31	38.5
Mid-shaft diameter Lat - R (9)	24				20.5		25
Mid-shaft diameter Lat - L (9)	24	21	19	25	23	24	25
Mid-shaft circumference - R	90				83		89
Mid-shaft circumference - L	85	91	75	98	88	87	90
Platycnemic index - R	81.35				70.68		69.23
Platycnemic index - L	80.00	65.62	70.37	67.56	71.87	77.4	67.50
Tibia-Femoral index - R							80.52
Tibia-Femoral index - L		86.97		86.91			

Table V, continued

Specimen No.	1973-IV	1972-IX	1972-X	1973-III	1972-XIII	1970-IV
Sex	M	M	M	F	F	M
Fibula:						
Maximum length - R (1)						
Maximum length - L (1)	417		427			
Mid-shaft diameter A-P - R (3-2)				14		
Mid-shaft diameter A-P- L (3-2)	16	15	17	14.5	13	
Mid-shaft diameter Lat - R (3-1)				11.5		
Mid-shaft diameter Lat - L (3-1)	15	13	13.5	11	17	
Mid-shaft circumference - R				47		48
Mid-shaft circumference - L	53	50	48	43	50	48

Table V, continued

Specimen No.	1973-II	1972-III	1973-IV	1972-X	1973-III	1972-XIII	1970-IV
Sex		M	M	M	F	F	M
Calcaneus:							
Maximum length - R (1)	84			84	79	78	79
Maximum length - L (1)	85	39		85	87	78	
Talus:							
Maximum length - R (1)	55		54	63		53	54
Maximum length - L (1)	55	58.5	63	64	54	54	55
Breadth - R (2)	48.5		56	44		39	39
Breadth - L (2)	49	44	52	44	42	39	39
Height - R (3)	30		35	38		29	
Height - L (3)	32	32	34	38	30	32	
Patella:							
Height - R (1)	43		46	46			40
Height - L (1)	44		44.5	47		40.5	40
Breadth - R (2)	46		48	45			46
Breadth - L (2)	47		45	47		40	44

TABLE VI. ESTIMATION OF STATURE FROM LONG BONES

Specimen No.	Sex	Measurements of maximum lengths in mm		Stature estimate cm	Stature estimate inches
1973-II	M	Humerus-L	357	180.40	71.02
		Radius-L	295	190.52	75.00
		Ulna-L	312	189.49	74.60
1972-II	M	Humerus-L	336	173.73	68.47
1973-IV	M	Humerus-R	363	182.25	71.75
		Humerus-L	361	181.63	71.51
		Radius-R	295	190.52	75.00
		Ulna-R	319	192.08	75.62
		Ulna-R	316	190.97	75.18
		Femur-L	499	180.17	70.93
		Tibia-L	434	187.98	74.00
1972-IX	M	Radius-R	265	179.18	70.54
		Ulna-R	295	183.20	72.12
		Femur-L	480	175.65	69.15
1972-X	M	Humerus-R	364	182.56	71.87
		Ulna-R	308	187.96	74.00
		Ulna-L	307	187.64	73.87
		Femur-L	512	183.26	72.15
		Tibia-L	445	190.76	75.10
1970-IV*	M	Humerus-R	328	171.00	67.30
		Radius-R	268	180.00	70.10
		Radius-L	266	179.00	70.40
		Ulna-R	288	181.00	71.20
		Femur-R	464	172.00	67.60
		Femur-L	462	171.00	67.30
		Tibia-R	391	177.00	69.50
		Tibia-L	390.5	177.00	69.50
1973-III	F	Humerus-R	348	174.89	68.85
		Radius-R	285	190.02	74.81
		Ulna-R	300	185.86	73.17
		Ulna-L	295	183.72	72.33
1972-XIII	F	Humerus-R	358	178.25	70.18
		Tibia-L	435	187.68	73.88

* A statue of 170.03 cm (68.51 in) is estimated for this specimen by Dutta (1973; Dutta *et al.* 1972) with reference to Trotter's tables of 1952 and 1958, but Dutta does not indicate which of the long bones were used in this determination of stature. Stature estimates in centimenters and inches for each of the long bones of this specimen and others are calculated by the present writers using formulae favored by Trotter (1970). Standard errors for these formulae are given in Table XXVIII of Trotter (1970: 77). These are in the neighbourhood of ± 3 to ± 4 cm.

TABLE VII. SUMMARY OF PATHOLOGIES AND ANOMALIES

Specimen No.	Osteological abnormality and diagnosis	Anomalous features and markers of habitual stress
1972-I	————	————
1973-II	Lipping on thoracic and lumbar bodies: osteoarthritis.	Squatting facets.
1972-II	Dental enamel hypoplasia on incisors and canines of upper and lower dentitions: marker of an episode of arrested growth.	Hyperdevelopment of muscular attachments for Anconeus and Supinator.
1973-IV	Lipping on thoracic and lumbar bodies: osteoarthritis. Lipping on right patella: local inflammation of knee joint.	Hyperdevelopment of muscular attachments for Anconeus and Supinator.
1972-X	Lipping on all vertebral bodies: osteoarthritis. Exostosis at distal end of right radius: osteochondroma. Exostosis of the left 1st metatarsal: osteochondroma.	Squatting facets. Hyperdevelopment of tendinous attachments to palmar surface of manual phalanges. Perforation of olecranon fossae of humerus. Hyperdevelopment of tibial tuberosity.
1970-IV	Depression of right frontal region: "left hemiperesis" (Dutta 1973; Dutta *et al.* 1972).	Squatting facets.
1973-III	————	Hyperdevelopment of muscular attach ments for Anconeus and Supinator.
1972-V	Lipping of 4th lumbar body: osteoarthritis.	Hyperdevelopment of muscular attachments for Anconeus and Supinator.
1972-XIII	————	————

SOCIO-ECONOMIC ASPECTS OF MEGALITHIC VIDARBHA

Ravi Moorti

Since the first systematic study by V.D. Krishnaswami (1949:35-45) on the classification and interpretation of south Indian megaliths we have a spate of publications on megaliths in various parts of India. Because of this, we have not only a fair idea of the distributional pattern of megalithic sites throughout India but also their typology and the material culture. Inspite of all this work, it is disappointing that we know so little about the socio-economic aspects of Megalith builders. For this lacuna not only are we responsible but also the nature of data that we have in our hands. The lack of habitation sites in most of the regions and very few objects connected with the material culture restricts our inferences and interpretations. However, one of the most noteworthy attempts to reconstruct the socio-economic aspects of Megalithic society is that of Lawrence S. Leshnik (1974).

In the present paper, however, I propose to analyse the data available for Vidarbha megaliths and throw some light on their socio-economic aspects. The reason for choosing Vidarbha region for the present discussion is that, not only very systematic explorations and excavations have been carried out in that area but also, most of the data have been published. Added to these, is the advantage of the three excavated habitation sites in that area.

THE REGION

The region of Vidarbha which forms the eastern and north-eastern part of Maharashtra is well known for its antiquity. It consists of eight districts of Maharashtra viz., the districts of Buldana, Akola, Amaravati, Yeotmal, Wardha, Nagpur, Bhandara and Chandrapur. To the east and northeast of the region occur the Gondawana series which are important because of their coal and manganese deposits. The region is boundec on the north by Khandwa, Betul, Chhindwara, Seoni and Balaghat districts, on the east by Durg and Jagdalpur districts of Madhya Pradesh, on the south by Parbhani, Nanded districts (of Maharashtra) and Adilabad district of Andhra Pradesh, on the west by Jalgaon and Aurangabad districts of Maharashtra, respectively. The relief features are characterised largely, by the residual hil ranges of the Satpuras and their detached members; enclosing between them are the undulating black soil valleys. Much of the topography is typically one of the Deccan trap having flat topped and terraced features, low buttressed sides and isolated knolls. Much of this undulating plateau is drained not only by the rivers Wain ganga, Wardha and their tributaries but also by the river Tapi and its tributaries in the western part of some extent. The average rainfall in the region is between 110-125 cms. Although, the region as a whole supports the monsoonal deciduous type of forests but they are found only in the more hilly parts of the region. Valleys are almost completely cultivated but the plateau forms anc residual hills of lower order support only scrub and poor grass land.

PROBLEM

Although there are numerous questions related with Megalithic people and their way of life, in the present paper, maninly two problems have been taken up for the discussion. The first is the nature of the economy of these people and their subsistence pattern. The second problem is related to the nature of their social organisation.

APPROACH

In the present paper, objects (particularly those found in the burials) have been considered according to their 'Technomic' or 'Sociotechnique' significance. Then, their quantitative distribution at each site has been analysed. It may be stated that the 'Technomic' items are the ones which are used as a tool for specific purpose (e.g. tools such as chisels, adzes, hoes and artifacts such as fishhooks, grinding stones, awls,etc.) The 'Sociotechnique' items are those which are retained by a person/persons and indicate his/ their social status and prestige in society. Scarcity of the material and its value are the two deciding factors in these items. Gold objects, specific weapons such as iron daggers with copper hilt, lids with finials (earthen and copper) and horse have been considered as 'sociotechique' items. The assumption here is that difference in the size of a monument as well as the total number of objects interred as burial furniture may indicate differences in the status of the persons in a society. Of the interred objects some may be prestigious and will fall in the category of 'sociotechnique' items.

NATURE OF DATA

In the following pages an attempt has been made to analyse the material evidence recovered from excavations at Takalghat-Khapa, Gangapur, Naikund and Mahurjhari, the detailed reports of which are available. Though few other sites have been excavated in this region such as, Kamptee (Pearse: 1872), Khaiwarra (Carey: 1871), Junapani (Rivett-Carnac: 1869, *IAR* 1961-62: 32-34) and Mandhal (*IAR* 1976-77: 39-40), these have not been considered for detailed discussion for want of published accounts, but wherever possible, inferences have been drawn from the available evidence.

The total number of megalithic sites discovered in Vidarbha region is 76. These occur throughout this region. All these monuments typologically belong to a single type, i.e. pits bounded by a stone circle except, for a few dolmens which have been noticed in Bhandara district. All the habitation (cum-burial) sites are located on river banks; the site of Takalghat on river Krishna, Naikund on the Pench and Bhagi Mahari on the Kolar. The distribution pattern here shows a thick cluster of sites in the Nagpur district which has nearly 70% of the total sites. Of the 50 sites brought to light so far, only three (i.e. Takalghat, Naikund and Bhagi Mahari) are habitation-cum-burial sites. In the present discussion Bhagi Mahari has not been considered because the work started only year ago and the report is awaited.

It is interesting that in Nagpur district all the sites are located within a radius of 45-50 kms. So the average distance between two sites is less than 2 kms.

At Mahurjhari (henceforth referred as MHR) where more than 141 stone circles were noticed, only 15 have been excavated. Of the total excavated, 14 have been considered for analysis as the remaining one (Meg. 1 of Loc. I) was disturbed. The largest stone circle at this site had a diameter of 16.45 mtrs. and the smallest 8.22 mtrs. Hence, 12.33 mtrs. was taken as a dividing line (average of the largest and smallest circle) between the bigger and smaller stone circles. Of the fourteen megaliths, nine fall under the former category and five under latter category. Two were double stone circles belonging to the first category. Naikund (henceforth referred as NKD) has nearly 70 stone circles, of which only 6 have been excavated. Except one (Meg. 1 of Loc II) others are single stone circles, the former being a triple stone circle. Among the single stone circles the diameter of the largest circle was 26.30 mtrs. and that of the smallest circle was 9.10 mtrs. Thus, 17.7 mtrs. was taken as the dividing line. Accordingly, two stone circles fell under the first category and three under the second. The triple stone circle comes under the former category. At the site Khapa (hence forth referred as KP) nearly 20 stone circles were discovered, of which 9 have been excavated. Except one (Meg. 8 of Cl. I) all of them were found to be undisturbed. All the stone circles, excavated and unexcavated are single stone circles. The diameter of the largest stone circle was 24.40 mtrs. and that of smallest one

11.40 mtrs. So, the dividing line at this site was 17.9 mtrs. Accordingly, only one stone circle comes under the category of bigger circles and the remaining seven fall under the category of smaller circles. The last site which has been considered for the present analysis is Gangapur (henceforth referred as GP). Here also nearly 20 stone circles were found. All these stone circles are of single stone circle type. Of these, three have been excavated. The diameters of the largest and smallest stone circles were 12.12 mtrs. and 9.6 mtrs. respectively. The dividing line between bigger and smaller stone circles came out to be 10.86 mtrs. Accordingly, two stone circles come under the first category and one in the second.

The total number of metal objects and the sitewise break up of tools belonging to different 'technomic' categories has been given Table 1. It will be seen that the total number of metal objects recovered from megaliths was 168 at MHR, 61 at KP, 46 at GP and 58 at NKD. The total number of tools connected with craftsmans' work [Technomic category (B)] were 20 (11.49%) at MHR, 10(16.12%) at KP, 6 (13.04%) at GP, and 20 (34.48%) at NKD. Implements connected with agricultural/ horticultural activities (Technomic Category (C), were found only at MHR and NKD; figures for the former is 2 (1.14%) and latter 1 (1.72%). Objects connected with fishery (Technomic Category (D) were found only at KP and GP. Figures for the former site were 2 (3.22%) latter 1 (2.17%).

Table 2 shows the percentage of bones of various animals found at TKG and NKD. The total number of bones collected from different layers was 288 at TKG and 315 at NKD. The percentage of cattle was 63.88 at TKG and 70.7 at NKD. Goat came second; its percentage being 15.27 at TKG and 9.8 at NKD. Next came buffalo, with 7.32 at TKG and just 2.8% at NKD. The percentage of pig was 6.25 at TKG and only 4.4 at NKD. TKG yielded only 0.35% of horse remains while NKD 4.1%. Faunal remains of the other animals were almost in negligible quantity except those of fowl (2.77% at TKG) sambhar (0.35% at TKG and 6.6% at NKD) and dog/wolf (2.5% at NKD).

Table 3 shows the frequency of occurrence of objects of each category found at MHR and the average number of objects per burial. In the bigger single stone circles the total number of metal objects (of gold, iron and copper) was 107. Besides 70 objects of pottery were found. It was 32 and 22 in the smaller single stone circles. The total number of metal objects in double stone circles was 32 and pottery and stone 26. The average number of gold objects per burial in bigger single stone circles was 2.71 and in smaller single stone circle 0.4. The average number of gold objects per burial in double stone circles was 2.0. The average number of iron objects per burial was 4.42 in bigger single stone circles, 5.2 in smaller single stone circles and 5.5 in bigger double stone circles. The average number of copper objects per burial was 8.14 in bigger single stone circles, 0.8 in smaller single stone circles and 8.5 in bigger double stone circles. No stone objects were found in bigger single stone circels. The average number of stone objects per burial was 0.6 in smaller single stone circles and 1.5 in bigger double stone circles. As regards pottery, the average number of pots per burial was 10.00 in bigger single stone circles, 4.0 in smaller single stone circles and 11.5 in bigger double stone circles.

The distribution pattern of various 'socio-technique' items and their frequency at MHR has been shown in Table 4. The average of horse remains per burial in single stone circles of both categories was 0.42. In bigger double stone circles it was 1.0. In bigger single stone circles the average number of horse equipment per burial was 3.28 and in bigger double stone circles it was 1.5. No horse equipments were found in smaller single stone circles. In case of bigger single stone circles as well as smaller single stone circles the average number of copper/earthen lids with finial was 0.42 and 0.2 respectively. In the bigger double stone circles it was 2.0. The average number of iron daggers with copper hilt in smaller single stone circles was 0.4. This was not found either in single or double stone circles of bigger category.

Table 5 deals with the data from KP megaliths. Here, stone circles belonging to bigger category yielded 19 metal objects (of iron and copper) and it was 42 in case of the circles of smaller category. The total number of different objects (viz., iron, copper, stone and pottery) found in bigger stone circles was 37 and in smaller stone circles 66. No gold objects were found in the circles of either category. The average number of iron objects per burial in the bigger stone circles was 10.00 and in smaller stone circles 3.57. The average number of copper objects per burial in case of bigger stone circles was 9.0 and in smaller stone circles 2.42. No stone objects were found in the stone circles falling under bigger category. These objects were found in the stone circles of smaller category and its average per burial was 0.14. The average number of pots per burial was 18.00 in stone circles of bigger category and 3.28 in stone circles of smaller category.

The distribution pattern of various 'socio—technique' items and their frequency at KP has been shown in Table 6 . It will be seen that the average number of horse remains per burial was 1.0 in bigger stone circles and 0.28 in smaller stone circles. The average number of horse equipment per burial in the bigger stone circles was 6.0 and in smaller stone circles 1.71. No gold objects were recovered in the stone circles of both categories. The same was the case with iron daggers with copper hilt. The average number of copper/earthen lids with finial per burial in bigger stone circles was 4.0 and in smaller stone circles 0.14.

Table 7 shows the frequency of different items and their average number per burial found at GP. Bigger stone circles yielded a total of 36 metal objects (viz., iron and copper) and smaller 10. The total number of different objects (viz., iron, copper and pottery) found in bigger and smaller stone circles was 48 and 12 respectively. Gold as well as stone objects were not found in the stone circles at this site. The average number of iron and copper objects per burial was 5.5 and 12.5 in bigger stone circles and 8.0 and 2.0 in smaller stone circles, respectively. The average number of pots per burial was 6.0 in bigger stone circles and 2.0 in smaller stone circles. Objects of 'sociotechnique' significance were not found in this site.

Table 8 and 9 deal with the data from NKD. As can be seen in Table 8 the total number of metal objects (viz., gold, iron and copper) found in bigger single stone circles was 23 and in smaller 22. The total number of different objects (viz., gold, iron, copper and pottery) in the bigger single stone circles was 52 and in smaller single stone circles it was 102. The total number of metal objects (viz., iron and copper) and the total number of different objects (viz., iron, copper and pottery) in triple stone circle was 13 and 50 respectively. The average number of gold objects per burial in bigger single stone circles was 0.5 and smaller single stone circles 1.33. No gold objects were found in the triple stone circle. The average number of iron objects per burial was 3.0 and copper objects 8.0 in bigger single stone circles. It was 3.33 and 2.66 in case of smaller single stone circles. The average number of the same per burial was 9.0 and 4.0 in the triple stone circle. None of the stone circles yielded stone objects. The average number of pots per burial was 14.5 in bigger single stone circles, 26.66 in smaller single stone circles and 37.0 in the triple stone circle.

Table 9 shows the distribution pattern and frequency of various 'sociotechnique' items found in the stone circles of both the categories at NKD. The average of horse remains per burial was 1.0 in the stone circles of both the categories. The figures for horse equipment were 0.5 per burial in bigger single stone circles, 2.33 in smaller single stone circles and 1.0 in the triple stone circle. The average number of gold objects per burial was 0.5 in bigger single stone circles and 1.33 in smaller single stone circles. No gold objects were found in the triple stone circle. The figures for copper/earthen lids with finials were 1.5 per burial in bigger single stone circles and 0.33 in smaller single stone circles and 1.0 in the triple stone circle. Iron daggers with the copper hilt were not found in any of the stone circles.

The analysis of pottery types of different wares found in burials shows that at MHR 24 types were represented in double stone circles (average 12.0 per burial), 36 in bigger single stone circles (average 5.14 per burial) and 21 in smaller single stone circles (average 4.2 per burial). At KP, there were 18 types of different wares in bigger stone circles (18.0 per burial) and only 24 types in smaller stone circles (average 3.42 per burial). The data for GP megaliths on this aspect was not available. At NKD it was observed that 38 types of different wares represented in the triple stone circle (38.0 per burial) and 41 types (average 20.5 per burial) and 87 types (average 29.00 per burial) in single stone circles of bigger and smaller category, respectively.

DISCUSSION AND CONCLUSIONS

First, let us consider the megalithic economy in Vidarbha.

At all the four sites considered for analysis, the percentage of tools connected with craftsmen [Technomic category (B)] were more compared to those connected with agricultural/horticultural activities [Technomic category (C)] and objects connected with fishery [Technomic category (D)]. Although it is not possible to pin point the tools connected with smithery and carpentry which have been included in the technomic category (B), some of them do reveal that they were for specific use. For instance, iron chisels with rectangular section with one end pointed (which was hafted) and the other bevelled (which was) evidently used as a working edge for carving or for making mortice holes in wood or for shaving the surface of wood. The evidence from Naikund habitational site where a circular hut (having an internal diameter of 4.9 mtrs.) was found to consist several post-holes all along its inner and outer periphery, the average diameter of post-holes was 12.4 cms. and in several of them disintegrated remains of wooden posts were found (Deo and Jamkhedkar, 1982: 9). Though it is a solitary evidence, this suggests ample use of wood for construction purposes and may explain the common occurrence of chisels.

The finding of a crucible (in Phase IB at TKG) and the recent discovery of an iron-smelting furnace at Naikund (Gogte, 1982: 52-55) may suggest that both Takalghat and Naikund were 'production centres' of metal objects. This is further supported by the fact that at both these sites the percentage of technomic category (B) items is relatively higher than the remaining two sites.

The evidence of agricultrual/horticultural activities comes only from Mahurjhari and Naikund. But even at these sites the percentage of implements connected with this activity was comparatively less. For instance, both the sites yielded only two hoes each. Of the two at Naikund, one comes from layer (3) of the habitation area. Also few stone weights of digging sticks were found at Naikund. Moreover, the occurrence of ancient grains at Naikund suggests that megalithic people here were agriculturists, but, to a limited extent. Naikund has yielded the remains of lentil, black gram, wheat and common pea (Kajale, 1982: 60-63). However similar data is not available from Takalghat.

Objects connected with fishery were found only at Khapa and Gangapur. The evidence in the form of terracotta net sinkers found in Phase B and Phase A of Takalghat corroborate the evidence.

However, the occurrence of faunal remains in all the phases in varying percentage at Takalghat (Rao, 1970: 60-72) and Naikund (Badam, 1982: 70-88) has thrown interesting light. We can easily deduce that among the animals reared by megalithic people a majority consisted of cattle and sheep/goat. This would suggest that their's was a semi-pastoral economy based on herding and stock-raising.

The second major problem posed by the Vidarbhan megaliths is the nature of social organisation. A detailed analysis of the evidence of burial furniture throws some light on this important aspect. It was observed that the number of different objects and their average per burial tends to be more in bigger single stone circles than smaller ones. This difference was quite marked in the burials of these categories at Mahurjhari, Khapa and Gangapur. Only at Naikund, there was much difference. However, the distributional pattern of various 'sociotechnique' items also confirms this difference in bigger and smaller single stone circles atleast at the first three sites. The bigger double stone circles at Mahurjhari had, not only more burial objects but also had more items of 'sociotechnique' significance than in the smaller single stone circles. This difference in the interment of burial furniture suggests the existence of social hierarchy. It can be tentatively infêrred that the persons blonging to the upper strata of society received more ceremonious burial than the others. This is also indicated by the construction of monuments of bigger size with more number of objects as well as prestige goods. However, it is quite likely that the difference in the number of objects in the stone circles of either category may also be due to the occurrence of the skeletal remains of more than one person.

It was quite significant that none of the stone circles belonging to the bigger category yielded stone objects. At Khapa and Gangapur no gold objects were found in the stone circles of either category. The occurrence of this precious metal at Mahurjhari and Naikund suggests that probably the people there were more affluent.

(Guidance and encouragement, in the preparation of this article has comeforth from my research supervisor, Prof. M.K. Dhavalikar. I am also thankful to Prof. S. B. Deo for allowing me to study the excavated material and also for his valuable suggestions. I sincerely thank Dr. M.L.K. Murthy and Dr. K. Paddayya for their useful suggestions).

ABBREVIATIONS

Obj. — Object/s

G — Gold Object/s

I — Iron Object/s

C — Copper Object/s

S — Stone Object/s

(.) — Single Stone Circle

((.)) — Double Stone Circle

(((.))) — Triple Stone Circle

REFERENCES

1. Badam G.L. 1982 "Faunal Remains from Naikund with Special Reference to Domestication" in *Naikund Excavations* (1978-80) Eds. S.B. Deo, and A.P. Jamkhedkar, Dept. of Arch. & Museums, Govt. of Maharashtra, Bombay, Appendix VII, pp. 70-88.

2. Carey, J. J. 1871 "Stone circles found near Khaiwarra, Wardha District", in *Proc. Asiat. Soc. Bengal,* pp. 238-39.

3. Deo, S.B. 1970 *Excavations at Takalghat and Khapa* (1968-69), Nagpur Univ., Nagpur.

4. *Gazetteer of the Nagpur District, Maharashtra State,* (Revised Edition), Maharashtra Govt., Bombay, 1966, pp. 1-15.

5. Gogte, V. Ḋ. 1982 "Megalithic Iron-Smelting at Naikund (Part I) Discovery by Three-probe Resistivity Survey" in *Naikund Excavations* (1978-80), Eds. S.B. Deo, and A.P. Jamkhedkar, Dept. of Arch. & Museums, Govt. of Maharashtra, Bombay, Appendix II, pp. 52-55.

6. "Excavations at Junapani, Dist. Nagpur" in *Indian Archaeology – A Review* 1961-62, pp. 32-34.

7. "Excavations at Mandhal, Dist. Nagpur" in *Indian Archaeology – A Review* 1976-77, pp. 39-40.

8. Kajale, M.D. 1982 "First Record of Ancient Grains in Megalithic Habitational Context from Excąvations at Naikund (1978 season), Dist., Nagpur, Maharashtra" in *Naikund Excavations* (1978-80) Eds. S.B. Deo and A.P. Jamkhedkar, Dept. of Arch. & Museums, Govt. of Maharashtra, Bombay, Appendix IV, pp. 60-63.

9. Leshnik, L.S. 1974 *South Indian 'Megalithic' Burials – A Pandukal Complex,* Franz Steiner,

Wiesbaden.

10. Krishnaswami, V. D. 1949 "Megalithic Types of South India", in *Ancient India*, No. 5, pp. 35-45.

11. Pearse, G.G. 1872 "Notes on the Excavation of a Stone circle, near Kamptee, Central Provinces of India" in *J.Ethno. Soc. London*. Vol. I, pp. 207-217.

12. Rao, V.V. 1970 "Skeletal remains from Takalghat and Khapa Excavations" in *Excavations at Takalghat and Khapa* (1968-69), Ed. S.B. Deo, Nagpur Univ., Nagpur, Appendix I, pp. 60-72.

13. Rivett-Carnac, J.H. 1869 "Prehistoric Remains in Central India" in *Proc. Asiat. Soc. Bengal*, pp. 1-16.

Table 1

TOTAL NUMBER OF DIFFERENT 'TECHNOMIC' ITEMS AT EACH SITE AND THEIR PERCENTAGE

Tech. Category	MHR	KP	GP	NKD
(B)	20(11.49%)	10(16.12%)	6(13.04%)	20(34.48%)
(C)	2(1.14%)	—	—	1(1.72%)
(D)	—	2(3.22%)	1(2.17%)	—
Total No. of metal objects recovered from Megs.	168	61	46	58

Legend: (B) Tools connected with craftsman's work (carpentry/Smithery)
(C) Implements connection with agricultural/horticulture activities
(D) Objects connected with fishery

Table 2

PERCENTAGE OF DIFFERENT ANIMAL REMAINS IN RELATION TO THE TOTAL NUMBER OF ANIMAL BONES

	TAKALGHAT*	NAIKUND**
Bos indicus (Cattle)	63.88%	70.7%
Capra hircus (Goat)	15.27%	9.8% (Sheep/Goat)
Bubalus bubalis (Buffalo)	7.32%	2.8%
Sus scrofa (Pig)	6.25%	4.4%
Ovis vignei (Sheep)	3.12%	—
Gallus sp. (Fowl)	2.77%	—
Rattus rattus (Rat)	0.69%	—
Equus caballus (Horse)	0.35%	4.1%
Cervus unicolor (Sambhar)	0.35%	6.6% (Deer)
Gaur	—	0.6%
Wild sheep/Goat	—	0.3%
Dog/Wolf	—	2.5%
Lagomorph (Hare/Rabbit)	—	0.9%

* Total number of bones collected at TKG : 288

** Total number of bones collected at NKD : 315

Table 3

FREQUENCY OF VARIOUS OBJECTS AT MAHURJHARI AND AVERAGE PER BURIAL

BIGGER STONE CIRCLES

Total No. of metal objects (G+I+C)	Total No. of objects (G+I+C+P)	Percentage of Gold objs.	Iron objs.	Copper objs.	Stone objs.	Pottery
(.)107	177	17.15	28.97	53.27	—	65.42
Av.per.Br.		2.71	4.42	8.14	—	10.00
((.))32	58	12.5	34.37	53.12	5.17	39.65
Av.per.Br.		2.0	5.5	8.5	1.5	11.5

SMALLER STONE CIRCLES

Total No. of metal objects (G+I+C)	Total No. of objects (G+I+C+S+P)	Percentage of Gold objs.	Iron objs.	Copper objs.	Stone objs.	Pottery
32	55	6.25	81.25	12.5	5.45	36.36
Av.per. Br.		0.4	5.2	0.8	0.6	4.0

Table 4

DISTRIBUTION OF VARIOUS 'SOCIOTECHNIQUE ITEMS AT MAHURJHARI AND AVERAGE PER BURIAL

BIGGER STONE CIRCLES

	Horse	Horse equipment	Gold objects	Copper/Earthen lids with finial	Iron dagger with copper hilt
(.)	3	23	19	3	—
Av.per. Br.	0.42	3.28	2.71	0.42	—
((.))	2	3	4	4	—
Av. per.	1.0	1.5	2.0	2	—

SMALLER STONE CIRCLES

Horse	Horse equipment	Gold objects	Copper/Earthen lids with finial	Iron dagger with copper hilt
3	—	2	1	2
0.42	—	0.4	0.2	0.4

Table 5

FREQUENCY OF VARIOUS OBJECTS AT KHAPA AND AVERAGE PER BURIAL

BIGGER STONE CIRCLES							SMALLER STONE CIRCLES						
Total No. of metal objects (I+C)	Total No of objs. (I+C+P)	Percentage of Gold objs	Iron objs	Copper objs	Stone objs	Pottery	Total No. of metal objs. (I+C)	Total No. of objs. (I+C+S+P)	Percentage of Gold objs	Iron objs	Copper objs	Stone objs	Pottery
(.)19	37	—	52.63	47.36	—	48.64	42	66	—	59.52	40.47	1.5	34.84
Av. per. Br.		—	10.00	9.00	—	18.00	Av. per Br.	3.57	2.42		0.14	3.28	

Table 6

DISTRIBUTION OF VARIOUS 'SOCIOTECHNIQUE ITEMS AT KHAPA AND AVERAGE PER BURIAL

	BIGGER STONE CIRCLES					SMALLER STONE CIRCLES				
	Horse	Horse equipment	Gold objects	Copper/Earthen lids with finial	Iron with hilt dagger copper	Horse	Horse equipment	Gold objects	Copper/Earthen lids with finial	Iron dagger with copper hilt
(.)	1	6	—	4	—	2	12	—	1	—
Av.per. Br.	1.0	6.0	—	4.0	—	0.28	1.71	—	0.14	—

Table 7

FREQUENCY OF VARIOUS OBJECTS AT GANGAPUR AND AVERAGE PER BURIAL

BIGGER STONE CIRCLES							SMALLER STONE CIRCLES						
Total No. of metal objects (I+C)	Total No of objs. (I+C+P)	Percentage of Gold objs	Iron objs	Copper objs	Stone objs	Pottery	Total No. of metal objs. (I+C)	Total No. of objs. (I+C+P)	Percentage of Gold objs	Iron objs	Copper objs	Stone objs	Pottery
(.)36	48	—	30.55	69.44	—	25.00	10	12	—	80.00	20.00	—	16.66
Av. per. Br.		—	5.5	12.5	—	6.0	Av. per Br.		—	8.00	2.0	—	2.0

Table 8

FREQUENCY OF VARIOUS OBJECTS AT NAIKUND AND AVERAGE PER BURIAL

BIGGER STONE CIRCLES							SMALLER STONE CIRCLES						
Total No. of metal objects (G+I+C)	Total No. of objects (G+I+C+P)	Gold objs.	Iron objs.	Percentage of Copper objs.	Stone objs.	Pottery	Total No. of metal objects (G+I+C)	Total No. of objects (G+I+C+P)	Gold objs.	Iron objs.	Percentage of Copper objs.	Stone objs.	Pottery
(.)23	52	4.34	26.08	69.56	—	55.76	22	102	18.18	45.45	36.36	—	78.43
Av.per.Br.		0.5	3.0	8.0	—	14.5	Av.per. Br.		1.33	3.33	2.66	—	26.66
((.))13	50	—	69.23	23.07	—	74.0							
Av.per.Br.		—	9.0	4.0	—	37.0							

Table 9

DISTRIBUTION OF VARIOUS 'SOCIOTECHNIQUE ITEMS AT NAIKUND AND AVERAGE PER BURIAL

	BIGGER STONE CIRCLES					SMALLER STONE CIRCLES				
	Horse	Horse equipment	Gold objects	Copper/Earthen lids with finial	Iron dagger with copper hilt	Horse	Horse equipment	Gold objects	Copper/Earthen lids with finial	Iron dagger with copper hilt
(.)	2	1	1	3	—	3	7	4	1	—
Av.per. Br.	1.0	0.5	0.5	1.5	—	1.0	2.33	1.33	0.33	—
(((.)))	1	1	—	1						
Av. per.	1.0	1.0	—	1.0	—					

IRON AND URBANIZATIONZ: AN EXAMINATION OF THE INDIAN CONTEXT

Dilip K Chakrabarti

I. THE URBAN GROWTH-PROCESS

The early urban growth in India falls into two periods. The first period is co-terminous with the mature Indus civilization which lasted between c.2900/2800 B.C. and c.2000 B.C. This dating is based both on the MASCA calibration of the available rediocarbon dates (Braunswig 1975) and an examination of the archaeological evidence of contact between the Indus valley and Mesopotamia during the pre-Sargonic period (Chakrabarti 1982). This dating demonstrates that the Indus civilization, instead of being a somewhat later contemporary of the Sumerian civilization, ran in a more or less parallel chronological course. The non-urban late Harappan phenomenon, however, seems to have survived well into the second millennium B.C.

It must be realized that when the mature Indus civilization was flourishing in its distribution area between the Makran coast and the upper *doab* and between Jammu and the Kim estuary on the Gujarat littoral, the rest of India was strictly non-urban. The cultures which may be said to be contemporary with the mature form of the Indus civilization are the aceramic and the early phase of the ceramic neolithic cultures of Kashmir, the Ghaligai neolithic and the succeeding levels in the Swat valley in the northwest, the Ganeshwar culture of northeast Rajasthan, the Ahar culture of southeast Rajasthan, the Kayatha culture of Malwa in Madhya Pradesh, the Sawalda horizon in the north Deccan or Maharashtra, the neolithic culture of the Raichur *doab* between the Krishna and the Tungabhadra in the south Deccan or Karnataka and the Chirand neolithic culture of the middle Ganges valley in Bihar. The chronology of the earliest group of cultures elsewhere in the subcontinent is a little uncertain, apparently falling in the second millennium B.C. bracket. This impression may, of course, be based on inadequate knowledge. For instance, the Allahabad University adduced strong evidence of an independent beginning of agriculture based on rice at Koldihawa in the Belan valley, U.P., in the 6th—5th millennia B.C. (Sharma *et al.* 1980). Moreover, the evidence of the domestication of cattle, sheep, goat, buffalo, etc. and the occurrence of grinding querns in the early Mesolithic context at such sites as Bagor (c 5000 B.C.) in Rajasthan, Adamgarh (c.5500 B.C.) in Madhya Pradesh and Sarai Nahar Rai (c. 8395 B.C.) in the middle Ganges valley, U.P. suggest that much regarding the beginning of agriculture in different parts of India is either unknown or inadequately understood.

However, it must be admitted that it is only in the post-mature-Harappan and non-urban second millennium B.C. that there is an abundance of well-understood archaeological data on agricultural communities in different parts of India. By the middle of the second millennium B.C. there was no major area of the subcontinent which did not possess established and effective agricultural communities, rich in their range of crops and amply indicative of a well-rooted adjustment with their respective ecological settings. The first half of the second millennium B.C. must be considered one of the most significant periods of Indian history because it is during this period that the basis of modern village India assumed its basic shape. The archaeological data are perhaps not as abundant as one would wish them to be, but there is absolutely no doubt about this cultural premise (for a general review of data, Agrawal 1982, Allchin and Allchin 1982; also, Chakrabarti 1980).

The second period of the early Indian urban growth is generally supposed to have begun around 600 B.C. This coincides with the beginning of the early historic period in the Gangetic valley, which is reflected in the archaeological record not merely by the appearance of fortified settlements like Champa, Kausambi and Ujjain but also by the introduction of the northern black polished ware (NBP) which may rightly be called the type-fossil of the early historic archaeological assemblage in northern India. In a different context the present author (Chakrabarti 1974) postulated three distinct phases of early historic Indian urban growth.

"The first phase corresponds to the sixth-fifth centuries B.C. Beginning primarily along a belt stretching from Champa and Rajagriha to Ujjayini through Kausambi, this soon included the upper Gangetic valley and the Indo-Gangetic divide. This was also the period when the Achaemenid annexation of the northwest might have given rise to an urban nucleus there. The third—second centuries B.C. seem to mark the next phase of growth. This period witnessed the further growth of settlements in the areas which already came within the urban fold in the preceding phase. The basic importance of this phase, however, seems to be the fact that during this period many new regions, where the precise beginning of early historic period is still uncertain, came to develop or was about to develop a clear and unmistakable urban base. The regions which fall in this category are the Punjab plains, Sind, lower Gangetic valley, Rajasthan, Gujarat, Maharashtra and Orissa. That was also the twilight period of early history in Mysore, Kerala, Madras and Andhra. The third and final phase of urban growth in our chosen period seems to have developed in the early centuries A.D., characterized by a general urban prosperity throughout the subcontinent. One also detects now the indisputable evidence of urban settlements in the areas like Mysore, Kerala, Madras and Andhra where the earlier evidence seems to be vague and doubtful" (Chakrabarti 1974:89).

A number of issues are related to the date of c.600 B.C., accepted for the beginning of the early historic urban growth in the Gangetic valley. First, the NBP has been found to go back to c.700 B.C. at the site of Sringaverapura in U.P. (Agrawal *et al*. 1981). This dating clearly indicates that the hitherto accepted date of c.600 B.C. for the beginning of the early historic period in the Gangetic valley is not an infallible and fixed point. Secondly, the precise date of the beginning of the early historic urban growth in this context also depends on the antiquity of early historic writing. This does not go beyond the Mauryan period as far as the direct archaeological evidence is concerned. Does it mean that for early historic India an urban situation can be postulated only from the third century B.C. onwards ? On the other hand, there are literary references to the tradition of writing on perishable materials in India long before the Mauryas. It is difficult to accept that the prose part of the later Vedic texts and the grammar of Panini (c.500 B.C.) were written without the benefit of writing. The generally accepted position is that the Brahmi script was produced in the seventh or eighth century B.C. (Allchin and Allchin 1982:360). Thirdly, the settlement size of some painted grey ware sites in the range of 9—10 hectares or more has been used to argue urban functions for some large painted grey ware settlements (Shaffer 1979). On the whole, there is a good case to take the beginning of the early historic urban growth beyond c.600 B.C. and put it around c.700 B.C., if not earlier. The overemphasis on the presence of fortifications, burnt brick houses, etc. to call a site "urban" has generally ignored the position of that settlement in the regional settlement size hierarchy. If this position justifies the assumption that the settlement in question fulfilled some urban functions (administrative, economic, etc.) in the regional landscape and if the contemporary society is literate, there is no reason why this settlement cannot be called urban, even if it is found to possess no fortification and burnt-brick architecture.

It must be stated forthwith that this early

chronology of the development of Gangetic cities is not acceptable to all scholars. For instance, although A. Ghosh (1973) dates some of the early historic fortifications around 600 B.C. he is unwilling to push back the antiquity of early historic writing beyond fourth-fifth century B.C. (Ghosh 1973:14). A more explicit theoretical position was taken by Niharranjan Ray (1978) in this regard. He is sceptical of the picutre of urban life in the early Buddhist texts not merely because these texts in their extant versions may be much later than the 6th century B.C. but also because the excavations at the urban sites mentioned in the early Buddhist literature have not revealed, by and large, any impressive structural remains during that period. The reason, according to him, lies in the fact that "the Ganga basin ... was still (that is, between c.600 B.C. and c.350 B.C.) in a *Jana* — stage of socio-political development passing through a long and arduous process of state formation" (Ray 1978:136). It is, of course, true that it is only with the Mauryas that the whole of India emerges into clear historical light. Even in the Gangetic valley whatever urban element there was in the preceding period got consolidated and assumed a sharper focus only under the *Mauryas*. Regarding the Gangetic urban centres Ray writes:

"Many of these places must have been, at the time of the Buddha and much later too, just *gamas* or *mahagamas* or at the most, agglomerated and fortified *jana* —settlements or *nigamas*, situated within realms which where headed by *jana*-kings or chieftains. ... It is not unlikely that the raising of a few such *gamas, mahagamas* and *nigamas* or agglomerated *jana*—settlements (like the one at Rajagriha) as were hallowed by their association with the Buddha and his immediate disciples, to city centres, may have been due first to Chandragupta's imperial design and later to Asoka's pilgrimage to those places" (Ray 1978:137).

Ray has a point but he has obviously overstated his case. The clue to urbanism is provided by the settlement hierarchy of a given period and, as we have emphasized, impressive structural remains are not safe criteria to judge whether a site was urban or not.

II. THE ROLE OF IRON

As far as the role of iron in this urban base is concerned, there is no gainsaying the fact that it was sustained by iron technology. For one thing, the position of copper as a technological element is marginal during this period, and for another, iron implements played an important role not merely in the contemporary agricultural and craft activities but also in the lay-out of the major new settlements. An unequivocal instance of this latter phenomenon comes form Ujjayini. N.R. Banerjee (1965) dates the beginning of the massive fortification around ancient Ujjayini in Malwa in 750-500 B.C. Ghosh (1973) prefers a central date of c.600 B.C. but he does not deny the possibility of an earlier dating. What is, however, important is that the body of the rampart was found to contain " a fairly well-preserved blade of an iron spade, and some indeterminate objects of iron, suggesting, by their length, crow-bars..." (Banerjee 1965:16). The beams of wood teak (*Tectona grandis*) and Safed Khair (*Acacia feruginea*) used in the revetment of the rampart along the Sipra on whose bank Ujjayini is located could have been cut and dressed only by iron implements. Moreover, as the present author (Chakrabarti 1976, 1979) has shown, by the time of the *satapatha Brahmana* (c.700 B.C.?) iron was a common enough metal to be associated with ordinary people. There is no reason to doubt that the early historic Indian urban base was sustained by iron technology.

But to what extent did it play a causative role in this urban transformation ? The issue is a theoretical one and must be closely examined. First, it may be useful to study the inventories of iron objects from the painted grey ware and NBP levels at Atranjikhera in Etah district, U.P. The virtue of the site is that it was extensively excavated under the inititative of S.Nurul Hasan of Aligarh University and a detailed report on these excavations has recently been published (Gaur 1983). In the Painted Grey Ware level Atranjikhera has yielded 135 objects and indeterminate pieces.

"The identifiable finds comprised fourteen kinds of objects, viz, arrowhead, spearhead, shaft, pair of tongs, clamp, chisel, bar (rod), borer. needle, hook, nail, axe, knife and bangle. One may broadly divide them into three groups: (i) weapons, (ii) craft tools and implements, (iii) household objects and ornaments. The presence of iron objects in such profusion and the discovery of furnaces, slag and certain specific tools used by blacksmiths, suggest that not only were iron goods manufactured at the site, but that the smelting of iron ore was also carried out here" (Gaur 1983 : 219—220).

The phase-wise break-up is as follows: the lower phase : 8; the middle phase : 46; the upper phase : 81.

In the succeeding NBP phase Atranjikhera has yielded a total number of 346 iron objects including indeterminate pieces. Apart from slag and indeterminate pieces there are 29 types – arrowhead, spearhead, shaft, sickle, spud, ploughshare, hoe, digger, tongs, clamp, ring-fastener, socketed clamp, staple, bolt, plumb-bob, nail, bar, hook, borer, chipping knife, chopper, pipe, scraper, chisel, axe, knife, lid, disc and bangle. The pahse-wise break-up is the following : Phase A : 147; Phase B : 79; Phase C : 70; Phase D : 50.

At this point it may be noted that agricultural implements, although unknown in the painted grey ware level at Atranjikhera, occur in this level at Jakhera (hoe and sickle), also in Etah district, U.P. (Sahi 1978). According to our opinion iron implements have been used in agriculture in the *Doab* and elsewhere right from the beginning of the first millennium B.C. Also, as the scientific analyses of the Atranjikhera painted grey ware iron objects (Gaur 1983: 487-489) indicate, the technique of carburisation by which a steely edge is obtained in wrought iron implements was known to the painted grey ware people. However, none of these two points, the presence of agricultural implements in the painted grey ware horizon and its familiarity with the technique of carburisation, detracts from the basic fact that the proper burgeoning of the iron industry had to wait till the NBP period (135 pieces in the painted grey ware level and 346 pieces in the N.B.P. level at Atranjikhera; 14 painted grey ware iron object types and 29 types of objects in the NBP level at this site). We would argue that the proper development of the iron industry is concommitant with the urban base; it does not significantly antedate it. It is useful to remember that technology increases in complexity only with social demands, although the technology itself may be known earlier.

The situation is what it should be. Till the early part of the 20th century there were innumerable groups of preindustrial iron-smelters all over the country outside the major alluvial stretches. Most of them fulfilled only the local needs for iron implements. In 1918 a preindustiral iron-smelting family was reported in the vicinity of the Tata steel works at Jamshedpur, Bihar. The following extract is interesting :

"They make ploughshares, sickles, arrowheads, axes, knives, and all domestic articles they require. On the average the family run one heat a week, taking the remainder of the time to attend to their farm, gather ore and wood, make charcoal, and make the iron into articles for sale" (MoWilliams 1920:162).

This family could also sell the object they made without leaving home. On the technological level they were pretty effective but socially and economically this effect cannot be visualized as highly significant. The basic iron technology practised by the preindustrial Indian iron-smelters till they became totally extinct in this century must have continued unchanged right from the period when the iron technology evolved and came of age in India. Historically, what matters in the Indian context is not the level of the technology itself but the social organization behind it.

The significant increase of iron object in NBP level at Atranjikhera is, in fact, logical because the scale of the society underwent a significant change in that period.

In the Indian context A. Ghosh wrote : " _ in a slow-moving society the impact of iron was slow. The metal did not produce any spurt in the material prosperity of the society" (Ghosh 1973:10). This is a view which has been strongly endoresed both by the present author (Chakrabarti 1973) and Niharranjan Ray (1978). The reason may also be brought home by referring to the preindustrial Indian iron-smelting furnaces. The most primitive type of these furnaces has been called the Kamar Joda furnace by W.F. Cleere who saw it in operation in 1963 and named it after the village in Singbhum district, with which it was associated (for the details, Chakrabarti n.d.). The Kamar Joda furnace was basically a shallow clay-lined bowl (1 ft. in diameter and 6 inches deep) dug in the earth. A mound of earth, 18 inches high, was raised above this bowl and extended for about 2 ft. behind it. A shaft, 3-4 inches in diameter, was made immediately above the centre of the bowl, the front of which was open. The whole structure was built with puddled clay mixed with chopped straw or husk. It was dried in the sun and cracks were lined with fresh clay. When the furnace was ready for operation, the bowl was filled with charcoal and the next step was to close the open front with damp sand, probably bonded with a little puddled clay. A tuyere was inserted through the sand wall and the blast was operated by using twin foot-operated bellows. About 30 pounds of ore were charged with an equivalent amount of charcoal. When the charge was used up the front wall was broken up and the bloom, a mass of slag and iron with much adhering unreduced ore and charcoal, was dragged out with tongs and quenched with water. The bloom was then battered with a hammer and the small fragments of metal were picked up by hand. The small pieces of iron were finally reheated and forged together. The ingot obtained from 30 pounds of ore weighed about 2 pounds. This, possibly, is the most primitive type of Indian iron-smelting furnace because there is no provision for tapping off slag in this type.

A more developed type of furnace was where slag could be tapped off during operation and the sponge could be taken out straight by opening the front of the furnace and be immediately hemmered into a tolerably sound bloom. In this type there was no necessity of hammering the sponge into small pieces, picking up the pieces of pure metal and reheating them into a bloom.

Both these types of furnaces must have been known to the early Iron Age Indian smelters. Whatever evidence we have (cf. Jodhpura, Atranjikhera, Naikund, etc.) points to this. What is important is that on this level of technology it is the scale of operation which matters. In the historic context the scale of operation could attain a significant magnitude only in the urban NBP level.

Along with this one must point out the strong element of continuity in cultural items from the chalcolithic to the Iron Age levels in India. This is not so marked in the *Doab* but elsewhere the chalcolithic elements like painted pottery, blade industry, etc. continue to occur in a significant quantity in the succeeding iron-bearing levels and demonstrate once again that the impact of iron technology was slow. It may also be emphsized that in many areas where iron technolgy began early (cf. south India, Berar, etc.) the transition to urbanism did not take place till a much later period. Obviously, the iron technology did not play a causative role in the urban transformation of these areas.

We are also of the opinion that the role of iron in the clearing of jungles in the Gangetic valley has been overemphasized. Two points have been noted by the present author elsewhere in this context (Chakrabarti 1983). First, there is no doubt a proliferation of sites in the painted grey ware period in contrast to the number of sites in the earlier black-and-red ware period. Two Ochre

Coloured pottery, five black-and-red and 17 painted grey ware sites were found in a survey in Aligarh district (information from M.D.N. Sahi). A survey of Kanpur district has yielded 46 painted grey ware sites in contrast to 9 black-and-red ware sites. The Kanpur data have been fully published (Lal 1984) and what clearly emerges is that the crucial break-off point in the settlment history of the region is the NBP ware phase when the number of settlements goes up to 99 and they are spread all over the district, sometimes away from the major rivers (the Ganga and the Yamuna) and their tributaries. That the NBP period provided a significant break-off point in the settlement history of the Gangetic valley has also been made clear by a recent survey of a part of Allahabad district including the area around Kausambi (Erdosy n.d.). The early urban period has here been visualized from c.700 to c.500 B.C., and although no significant increase is observed in the number of sites, this period is notable for the development of a clear settlement hierarchy with urban centres at their apex.

Secondly, the agricultural base of the Gangetic valley was laid down by the pre-iron farmers of the region. The present author (Chakrabarti 1983) has shown that the introduction of iron in the Gangetic valley did not lead to the introduction of a single important new crop to the earlier chalcolithic crop-pattern.

The Gangetic valley urbanization was no doubt due to a complex interaction of several factors _ a local agricultural base, an organized trading activity and a centralized political power-structure. If any single factor has to be given primacy, that should be given to the factor of political power and centralization. The economic and commercial activities may be important on their own account but can be effective only within the framework of a broader societal power structure (Chakrabarti 1972-73).

III. SUMMARY OF THE ARGUMENT

Beginning with a discussion on some of the major issues of the early Indian urban growth, the present paper has tried to argue that the beginning of iron technology did not play a causative role in the early historic urban transformation, although the iron technology had no doubt sustained it. The proper burgeoning of the iron industry was concommitant with, and not earlier than, the urban growth as evidenced in the NBP period. The slow impact of iron technology in the Indian context has been driven home by referring to preindustrial iron-smelting furnaces surviving till the 19th and the early part of the 20th centuries. Moreover, it has been emphasized that the agricultural base of the Gangetic valley was laid down by the pre-iron farmers and that no important new crop was added after the introduction of iron. It has also been surmised that the urbanization of the Gangetic valley owed perhaps more to the growth of organized political power structures in the region around or before 600 B.C. than to such factors as economic and commercial activities.

REFERENCES

Agrawal, D.P., Bhandari, N., Lal, B.B. and Singhvi, A.K. 1981 Thermoluminiscence dating of pottery from Sringaverapura - a Ramayana site. *Proc. Indian Acad. Sci. (Earth Planet. Sci.)*. 90 : 161-172.

Agrawal, D.P. 1982 *The Archaeology of India.* London.

Allchin, B. and F.R. 1982 *The Rise of Civilization in India and Pakistan.* Cambridge.

Banerjee, N.R. 1965 *The Iron Age in India.* Delhi.

Braunswig, R.H. 1975. Radiocarbon dating and the Indus civilization : calibration and chronology. *East and West.* 25 : 111-145.

Chakrabarti, Dilip K. 1972-73 Concept of the Urban Revolution and the Indian context. *Puratattva.* 6 : 27-32.

Chakrabarti, Dilip K. 1973 Beginning of iron and social change in India. *Indian Studies : Past and Present.* 14 : 329-338.

Chakrabarti, Dilip K. 1974 Some theoretical

aspects of early Indian urban growth. *Puratattva*. 7 : 87-89

Chakrabarti, Dilip K. 1976 The beginning of iron in India. *Antiquity*. 50:114-124.

Chakrabarti, Dilip K. 1979 Iron in early Indian literature. *Journal of the Royal Asiatic Society*. 22-30.

Chakrabarti, Dilip K. 1980 Early agriculture and the development of towns in India. *Cambridge Encyclopedia of Archaeology* (ed. A. Sharratt). Cambridge. 162-167.

Chakrabarti, Dilip K. 1982 "Long barrel-cylinder" beads and the issue of pre-Sargonic contact between the Harappan civilization and Mesopotamia. *Harappan Civilization : A Contemporary Perspective* (ed. G. Possehl). Delhi. 265-270.

Chakrabarti, Dilip K. 1983 The issues of the Indian Iron Age. Key paper in the seminar of "Recent advances in Indian Archaeology". Deccan College, Pune.

Chakrabarti, Dilip K. n.d. Preindustrial Indian iron. *Indian Horizons* (forthcoming).

Erdosy, G. n.d. Settlement archaeolgy of the Kausambi region. *Man & Environment* (forthcoming).

Gaur, R.C. 1983 *Excavations at Atranjikhera*. Delhi.

Ghosh, A. 1973 *The city in Early Historical India*. Simla.

Lal, Makkhan 1984 Summary of four seasons of explorations in Kanpur district, Uttar Pradesh. *Man & Environment,* VIII.

McWilliams, A. 1920 Indian iron making at Mirjati, Chotanagpur. *Journal of the Iron and Steel Institute* : 160-167.

Ray, N.R. 1978 Technology and Social change in early Indian history.*Puratattva* No. 8

Sahi, M.D.N. 1978 New light on the life of the painted grey ware culture as revealed from excavations at Jakhera (dist. Etah). *Man & Environment*. II: 101-103.

Shaffer, J.G. 1979 Bronze Age iron from Afghanistan: its implications for south Asian protohistory. Mimeographed.

Sharma, G.R. *et al.* 1980 *Beginnings of Agriculture*. Allahabad.

FROM COPPER TO IRON

Vibha Tripathi

Recent studies all over the world, mainy by way of researches in ancient technology, demand a fresh look at the metallurgical developments during the transitional phase from copper/bronze to iron in India.

Studies in Indian iron age are still lacking on the subject of technique of iron smelting and forging. But work on the subject is in progress at serveral places outside India. Metallurgists like Smith Maddin, Tylecote, Muhley, Charles, etc., just to name a few, are actively engaged in finding out an answer to the question as to how the earliest metallic iron made its appearance and under what circumstances. (We shall not take into account the meteoric iron or unsmelted iron here as it has little contribution to make towards the beginning of the regular use of iron as a metal). The conditions might not have been too divergent from one part of the world to another in the bronze age communities of 3rd-4th millennium. It is fully justifiable therefore to take a stock of the existing data on the ancient iron technology in other parts of the world and to see how it works in Indian context.

In dealing with the issue we have to address ourselves to certain querries concerned mainly with technique of manufacture. Could the technique of making iron evolve into the existing furnaces with the limited know-how of metal craft? Was it an accidential by-product of copper working ? Or circumstances forced a deliberate search for an alternative raw material for substituting copper/bronze, rather a scarce and expensive metal ? Did early historic man accidentally come across metallic iron in the vicinity of rich and high quality ore deposits ?

These questions if answered convincingly would solve the problem of the emergence of iron as a useful metal. There was much more than a mere familiarity of man with iron ore that was needed to usher in a regular production of metallic iron which is one of the most common mineral deposits of earth's crust. We have to explore and reconstruct the possible conditions which heralded its use in different parts of the world.

Metallurgy, which includes the knowledge of ore smelting, forging, etc., began sometimes in 6th-5th millennium. B.C. Copper and bronze were manufactured into tools and implements effectively showing thereby a thorough understanding of the metallurgical processes. At several centres, notably in West Asia, copper/bronze tools begin to play an important role in cultural process. Gold, silver, lead, etc. were also picked up and shaped into ornamental objects.

At this very stage of development we come across stray occurrences of iron objects. The earliest reference to iron comes from Anatolia from the Old Assyrian period (3rd millennium). Generally iron makes its earliest emergence in form of bi-metallic objects as an embellishement in gold or copper/bronze implements. Daggers or knives of ceremonial importance were inlaid with iron stubs or pins. In rare cases ornaments like beads or pins or other luxury goods were fashioned out of iron. It is also known to have been used for medicinal and magico-religious purposes. Some such objects are reported from Afghanistan from 3rd millennium context (Shaffer, 1984) discussed below. The use and availability of iron was scarce and restricted to the nobility of the copper/bronze Age. It is thus accepted that iron began to be recognized as a distinct metal. At best it could have resulted from accidental smelting in a form of spongy bloom from which some iron was squeezed by means of hammering. This explains the scarcity of iron at this stage even in the Hittite country in 13th cent. B.C. (e.g. Letter from Hattusilis III to Ramses II; Gurney 1961: 83). While the presence of iron as a distinct metal was recognized, the emergence of iron metallurgy had to await several centuries.

On this basis, the metallurgists have postulated the possible course of events which converted the accidental iron into a regular metallurgical feat.

To examine whether it was feasible to produce iron accidentally in camp fires or kilns or the like, Coglan as far back as 1955-56 worked on these lines but the results were rather unencouraging. He worked with a variety of ores working in open camp fires but it invariably lead to roasted ore or cinder.

Smelting of iron, however, had to await mastery in pyrotechnology, especially of sophisticated blast furnaces, capable of attaining high temperature, at least upto 1200 ^{0}C. Equally essential prerequisite was an effective and efficient use of fluxes. Iron if present in any form, either accidentally or deliberately (as flux) would result into a bloom which can lead to metal extraction. Thus iron is said to be an inevitable technical by-product of copper and lead smelting: Iron was directly involved as a flux in the development of consistent technique of smelting silicious ores (Wertime 1980: p.3).

To further reinforce this, Wertime alongwith Smith conducted an actual field experiment in iron at Anjileh near Yazd in a tradtional clay and straw built furnace which was fueled with charcoal. They discovered that for 6 kg. of cerussite ore, 150 gm of haematite was being used a flux. The furnace had goat skin bellows, a square section, a height of 8 ft. and a tapering shaft. Near this furnane was discovered a salamander or 'bear' of iron of a very big size. This was a 3000 pound ball of metallic iron, an actual by-proudct of copper smelting furnace. Smith suggests, quoting Percy (1861:423. 431), on this basis that iron may have originated in copper smelting,for copper smelting furnaces also produce, bears, under certain conditions. It has to be brone in mind though that it is an *incorporation*[1] of constituent for an *effect* rather than for a *product.* It demonstrates a growing understanding of the behaviour of materials in fire and how their behaviour might be controlled. More than this, however, it can clearly indicate an origin of production of metallic iron (Charles, 1980: 165). This may be possible only if certain preconditions are fulfilled,*viz.*

That the activity of iron oxide, added to the copper ore as flux, was high due to the lower percentage of silica and other gangue material present in the charge which readily reacts with iron oxide to form a slag having lower fusion temperature. Thus it created a condition for the simultaneous reduction of iron oxide which has resulted in the presence of streaks of iron in copper tools.

There is another possibility that iron oxide got reduced by solid carbon or carbon monoxide gas before it could react with silica, etc. to form fayalite and other slags and thus it got added to the molten copper metal. On solidification it got embedded as thin streaks in copper metal. This will change the colour of copper and also make it hard to cold work. Tylecote and Milton (1980:189, 1976, 24-33) have reported many magnetic copper objects showing the presence of iron therein. (It is significant here to point out to the fact that Rangpur and Ahar copper objects are reported to have a high percentage of iron. Almost in all analysed) copper objects from Rangpur: iron is found to be present, in some of them it is as high 1.88% (Excavation at Rangpur- *Ancient India* No. 19,p. 153. Dr. B.B. Lal). Commenting on Ahar copper objects Hedge *(Excavations at Ahar,* 1968:225, 22%) has reported 6.48 p.c. iron in a sample.

It might have also have been possible that in furnace reaching a temperature of 1200^{0}C or more, iron gets seperated as spongy lump when copper becomes molten.

Use of large amount of iron oxide would also lead to production of iron sponge. This is quite ductile in red hot condition (above 900^{0}C) and it can be easily hammered into desired shape. On cooling it would not be red but black and harder than copper. Thus iron was recognised as a metal.

1. These points brought out by Prof. Bhanu Prakash of Metallurgical Engineering Department, Banaras Hindu University, in course of our discussions on the subject.

Situation was thus ripe by the end of Bronze Age when iron as metal could appear. The smelting furnaces were improvised for casting copper, the use of fluxes was prevalent and there was a greater control of combustion and heat conservation. All this lead to an *INCREASED Incidence* of metallic iron occurring in the spent charge material and associated with the solidified copper. Eventually there developed an upsurge of interest in the iron for its own sake." (Charles 1980, 167).

From this general background we proceed to examine the specific situation in Indian subcontinent. The earliest metals are reported here from pre/early Harappan phase and from then on it is a continuous story. Copper objects from Harappan period reported by Agrawal (1971: table 14, 131) are quite pure ranging between 82 to 97 percent pure and so are the Copper Hoard objects. Their iron content is almost nil. Hegde in his recent paper (1985) has reported the presence of mining pits of chalcolithic period in Aravalli Hills. These deposits are also associated with gossans present as cap on copper ores. It is rich in iron oxide, particularly limonite which acts as an effective flux for copper smelting and is readily available with copper deposits. Hedge, on the basis of ore composition and softness of mines feels that these were the mines used by chalcolithic folk. Timber support from a gallery at 120 metres at Rajpur Dariba mines of Udaipur is dated by C^{14} to 3120 $\pm$ 168 B.C. (last quarter of 2nd millennium). It may be worth while analysing the copper objects of chalcolithic cultures form this area. Objects from Rangpur (see table) and Ahar have a fair trace of iron, almost in all analysed samples being fairly high in certain cases.

Table

Sample No.	No.	Description	Copper	Iron
5.	330	Copper pin	91.80	1.88
6.	442	Copper pin	96.60	1.86
7.	260	Copper pin	96.66	1.40
15.	525	Copper knife	59.60	1.08

(From Excavations at Rangur Etc. *Ancient India* No. 18-19,153).

The two objects from Ahar, analysed by Hegde (Sankalia, *et al.* 1969: 225, 228) show 6.48 and 1.22 per cent iron in finished copper objects. The slags from which the copper objects have been manufactured contain 48.26, 43.89 and 45.32 percent iron oxide which is a pretty high percentage. It suggest the use of chalcopyrite ore at Ahar. The metal extraction is not very perfect and iron is extracted along with copper. Hedge has pointed to this fact after analysing the axe which is a cast object. However, he does speak of the common usage of flux, etc. (Hegde, 1969:228). Due to such inadequacy in copper smelting and use of iron oxide as flux, copper objects are found to contain streaks of iron with cast copper objects. In such cases and in absence of sufficient control, iron would be dissolved by molten copper, leading to production of metallic copper (described above).

It is opportune at this stage to take into account the earliest occurence of iron in India. Here the reported occurrence of iron from south Afghanistan, a region contiguous and contemporary to the Indus Civilization is interesting indeed. Shaffer (1984:41-62) has tried to draw and focus the attention of scholars on *Bronze Age iron artifacts.* Chronologicallly, it corresponds well with mature Harappan phase. Mundigak (Casal-1961) Deh Morasi Ghundai (Dupree 1963) and Said Qala Tepe (Shaffer, 1971:72 & 78) are the sites supplying us with the above data. He has referred to two catagories (1) distinct and (2) indistinct objects. The first catagory includes just a few decorative iron (?) buttons studded in handles of mirrors and shafts, and one small iron ball acting as a clapper in a bell shaped pendant of bronze. The second, indistinct category makes a reference to natural iron nodules of varying sizes with extremely high iron content.

The above evidence merely indicates the familiarity of the above mentioned Bronze Age communities with iron ore; nothing beyond. At the most we can say that they had recognised and used iron ores for its weight and colour and also for magico-religious purpose as at Deh Morasi Ghundai the nodules came from the shrine complex. Though I agree with the view that iron technology evolved indginously in India and its neighbourhood but to use such an evidence of unsmelted iron to prove this point is totally unjustifiable. Either iron oxide was being used as flux in copper smelting or an iron rich ore like chalcopyrite was exploited by Harappan copper smiths (see Rangpur table) thus explaining its presence on the sites mentioned by Shaffer.

This brings us to the question of the reported occurrence of iron at Ahar from the Chalcolithic levels assignable to ca. 1300 B.C. Apparently this is the earliest occurrence of iron so far known and Sahi (1970: 365-68, 1980) is right in high lighting its significance. But in the light of what we have discussed above we can postulate that :—

1. In the absence of analysis one cannot be too sure if the specimens in question are of iron or iron-rich copper.

2. The objects are a result of accidental production of copper smelting as they were dealing with iron-rich copper ore like chalcopyrite and / or using iron oxide as a flux. Thus there exists a possibility that they are results of iron oxide. Nevertheless, the ancient Aharians had reached a stage to have realized the existence of a seperate metal whether they were able to exploit it as such, is a different matter.

3. The third alternative, as pointed out by Sahi, is that iron in Ahar is a genuinely distinct metal having come about as a by-product of the prevailing copper technology. This would *interalia* imply that the recognition of iron as a distinct metal had preceded the use for making finished objects. A reference has already been made in the preceding paragraph about this kind of experimentaion at the time of the extraction of copper from chalcopyrite ore. This can lead to an accidental production of metallic iron as evidenced into nearly 7% iron in an object analysed from Ahar (above).

For other parts of India, however, we have to visualize different situations.

1. In an area geologically rich in iron ore, man is bound to familiarize himself with the metallic properties of the 'stone', i.e. iron ore deposits which he is using in his day-to-day life. Such is the case in southern parts of Africa where Iron Age follows immediately after Stone Age without an intermediary Copper-Bronze age (Merwe 1980: 464). A similar situation may have existed in the Vidarbha region where iron is found from the very beginning (e.g. Takalghat, Khapa, etc.) of the cultural habitations.

2. In those regions where only an elementary knowledge of metals is attested to, there exists a probability of erroneous selection of ores (as both copper and iron ores have reddish colour). This will lead to an accidental discovery of spongy bloom of iron which could be easily hammered out and shaped into useful objects. Perhaps this is what made Tylecote (1980:211) comment, "iron smelting was not invented by advanced copper smelters but by more primitive copper-smelters". Rich iron ores are abundantly available in most parts of India. The beginning of iron at Tadkanhalli, Hallur, Eran, Chirand, etc. might be cases on the point. On analysis of iron objects from the former O.P. Agrawal (1983:98) restates the fact that it was extracted directly by the bloomery process.

3. Where copper smelting was quite well known there might be an accidental stumbling on some form of a metallic iron through copper smelting, e.g. at Ahar and Jodhpura, etc. in Rajasthan where existed a plethora of copper using cultures before iron came on the scene.

Thus depending on specific situations iron might have come about independently in several parts of India. (This point has been taken up in detail by the author elsewhere, (Tripathi, in press).

There remains little doubt that pyrotechnology was well advanced and the metallurgists were well equipped and fairly advanced during the Bronze Age in India. Furnaces were sophisticated enough to attain high temperature to melt copper/bronze. Fluxes were used for better and more effective extraction of metal. Use of iron oxides as a flux for copper is well attested to. It has in several cases even lead to resonably recognizable percentage of iron in copper which would further harden the finished objects. Such situations and several others, discussed above, might have helped recognition of iron as a metal, then to experimentations, later to its widespread use. We can't presumably argue that it was the scarcity of tin, etc. as has been shown to be the case in other parts of the world (Maddin 1975:63) which led to the search for an alternative metal in India; copper/bronze had always been used here only in a restricted amount.[1] Copper Hoards with heavy tools and implements might appear to be exceptions. But the very fact that they were invariably preserved into hoards is not without significance here. The common man seems to be confining himself to stone, clay, or some perishable material like wood, etc. That explains why iron in its early stage does not substitute copper but just makes a very slow emergence spanned over hundreds of years, having a negligible impact on the economic scene. Though the experimentations must have been a hard, arduos and time consuming process but must have been inevitable to come. Nevertheless it was a big leap as far as the growth of technology of that age is concerned, and slowly but gradually this new technological advance succeeded in bringing about economic, social and political trasformations.

REFERENCES

Agrawal, D.P. 1971 *The Copper Bronze Age in India,* Delhi.

Agrawal, O.P. 1983 *Puratattva,* Vol. 12. p. 98.

Casal, J.M. 1961 *Fouelles de Mundigak,* Paris.

Charles, J.A. 1980 'The coming of Copper and Copper Alloys and Iron : A Metallurgical Sequence'. *The Coming of the Age of Iron,* ed. Wertime and Muhly, Yale University Press.

Dupree, L. 1965 'Deh Morasi Ghundai: A chalcolithic site in south-central Afghanistan' *Anthropological papers of the American Museum of Natural History* 50;59-135

Gurney, 1961 Quoted by Sahi (1980, mentioned below)

Hegde, K.T.M. 1968 in *Excavations at Ahar,* Sankalia *et al.* Poona.

1985 Scientific Studies in Indian Archaeology: Paper read at Seminar on 'Recent Advances in Indian Archaeology, Pune. p. 100-109.

Lal (Dr. B.B.) 1963 Excavations at Rangpur & other Explorations in Gujrat *Ancient India,* No. 18-19.

Maddin, R. *et al* Muhly D., Wheeler T.S. *How the Iron Age Began.*

Merwe, N.J. Vonder 1980 Advent of iron in Africa ed. Wertime & Muhley (*op, cit,*)

Percy, J. 1964 *Matallurgy: Iron & Steel* London.

Sahi, M.D.N. 1979 'Iron in Ahar' *Essays in Indian Protohistory.* ed. Agrawal D.P. and Chakrabarti, D.K., Delhi

1980 Origin of Iron Metallergy in India, Paper presented at Indian History congress.

Shaffer, J.C. 1984 'Bronze Age Iron from Afghanistan', *Studies in the Arch. & Palaeoanthropology of South Asia,* ed. Kennedy and Fass Amer. Inst. of Indian Studies. New Delhi. 41-62.

1971 *Preliminary Field Report on Excavations at Said Qala Tepe, Afghanistan* : 24.89-127.

1972 *Prehistoric Baluchistan,* a systematic approach. Ph.D. Dissertation Univ. of Wisconsin.

1980 Tylecote R.F. 'Furnaces, crucibles & slags' in ed. Wertime & Muhly.

Tripathi, V. (In press, unpublished paper) Early Indian Iron—A Techno-Ethnological Angle.

WHEN DID UDAYANA RULE ? IN THE SIXTH CENTURY B. C. OR THE SIXTEEN CENTURY A. D. ? AN ASSESSMENT OF THE DATING OF THE PALACE-COMPLEX AT KAUSAMBI

B. B. Lal

Kausambi, located on the left bank of the Yamunā in District Allahabad, Uttar Pradesh, is one of the most noteworthy sites of the early historical times in the country. According to ancient literature, it was visited by the Buddha when Udayana was its ruler. Since the Buddha is known to have attained Nirvana in 487 B. C. (or 483 B.C.), it would not be unreasonable to assume that Udayana was ruling at Kausambi towards the end of the sixth century B.C. or some time there-bouts.

The University of Allahabad, under the direction of Professor G. R. Sharma, carried out extensive excavations at this site in the fifties and early sixties and, amongst other structures, brought to light a stone-built palace which the learned Professor ascribed to King Udayana (*Indian Archaeology 1960-61 – A Review* p. 34). This created a stir amongst archaeologists and historians, since the question was not confined to Kausambi or Udayana alone, but had a great import in so far as the history of architecture in India was concerned. Understandably, the discovery began to be looked upon with a degree of reserve.

While re-examining the defences around Kausambi in 1982 (cf. *Puratattva,* no 11, pp. 88-95), the present author also had a thorough look at the palace-complex located in the south-western part of the site. He got evidence of various kinds, internal as well external, to indicate that the palace-complex may be a medieval one. In March 1983, along with Shri M.N. Deshpande, Professor B.P. Sinha and Shri K.N. Dikshit, he visited the site once again. This time still more evidence came to light, confirming the fear that after all the palace may have nothing whatsoever to do with Udayana. The visiting team also included some staff members of the Archaeological Survey of India, viz. Shri Lal Singh, Surveyor, and Shri Birbal, Photographer, both of the Excavations Branch II, and Shri B.P. Maurya, a member of the conservation staff of the Mid-eastern Circle.

However, before the author records in detail the evidence just hinted at, he would first like to place before the readers what Professor Sharma has himself observed about the palace-complex. The description in *Indian Archaeology 1960-61 _ A Review* reads as follows (p. 34) :

> As excavated the palace-remains attest to three main phases of architectural evolution. Though the general lay-out remained more or less the same in all the three phases, the walls in the earliest were built entirely of random rubble, huge undressed stones being set in lime-mortar (pl. LVII A). Perhaps the wall-faces were plastered.
>
> In the second phase (pl.LVA), dressed stones, with an average size of 66x53x20 cm., were used for the facings; the core, however, remaining of rubble. The phase, indeed, represents the apogee of architectural excellence.
>
> In the third phase, which followed an extensive destruction of the palace, the walls were no longer built of stone alone. The core was made of bricks, while dressed stones were used for the facings. The corner-towers (pl. LVII B) were rebuilt and enlarged, the longest cross-section of one of them measuring nearly 19 metres. In the case of these towers, the base was of stone, and the upper part of stone and brick, used indiscriminately. Another noteworthy feature of this phase was the use of thick coatings of lime-plaster.
>
> It was observed that the random-rubble walls of the first phase were built prior to the Northern Black Polished Ware. The walls of the second phase came into being immediately after the occurrence of that Ware. The end of this phase was marked by a destruction of the palace. The walls and tower were razed to

the ground. There is also evidence of conflagration. The debris-layer yielded, besides sherds of the N.B.P. Ware, a sealing bearing an inscription, *ma (?) ha* (?)*rajasa* (?) A (?) *sagho...,* in characters of *circa* second century B.C. During the third phase, which witnessed a great building activity, evidently to make up for the destruction, the N.B.P. Ware was on the decline. In the upper levels of the phase occurred certain pottery-types in red ware, which, on the evidence of other early historical sites, may be dated to the beginning of the Christian era. According to the stratigraphic evidence, therefore, the origin of the palace goes back to *circa* 600 B.C., if not earlier. *It is, thus, not unlikely that it was occupied by king Udayana, the renowned contemporary of Buddha.* It seems to have been deserted after the fall of the Mitra dynasty.

The work was continued in 1961-62, of which the relevant details are also given below (*Indian Archaeology 1961-62 ---- A Review* pp. 50-52):

This year's excavation was intended primarily to lay bare the complete plan of the palace-complex during different periods of occupation and as such was horizontal in nature. The three-fold sequence of architectural evolution, as revealed last year, was on general grounds confirmed, the earliest phase being further divided into two Sub-phases corresponding to Phases I and II of the defences. It may be recalled that Phase I there, represented by a 1.27-m thick deposit, preceded the appearance of the Northern Black Polished Ware at the site.

Phase I A of the palace-complex yielded pottery-types like the dish-on-stand with a corrugated stem and in other forms, vaguley resembling those obtaining from the post-Harappan chalcolithic sites in western and central India. While some of them were painted in black on the red surface (pl LXXXII A), others were decorated with incised designs (pl. LXXXII B), similar to those from Onaur and Unchadih (1959-60, pl XLVII).

A huge structure, the exact nature of which is difficult to ascertain at this stage, also belonged to this Sub-phase. Bottle-shaped pots placed face downwards in parallel lines at one end of this wall provided interesting evidence, possibly of some ritual, in connection with the building of the place.

The next Sub-phase was marked by the use of the grey, both painted and plain, and red wares. The foundation of the stone palace was laid early in this Sub phase (pl. LXXVIII A). Out of the five layers which accumulated against the wall of this Phase, four preceded the N.B. P. Ware. The first phase of the palace, therefore, could be dated to *circa* eighth century B.C.

Phase II of the palace, associated with the use of the Northern Black Polished Ware, represented by the south-eastern tower on the Yamuna (pl. LXXVIII B), the western boundary-wall above the foundation of the wall of Phase I A and a drain of dressed stone.

Ascribable to Phase III of the palace were the extensive structures which in their ruins constitute two prominent mounds on the Yamuna. These structures were divided into three blocks enclosing two galleries running north-south (pl.LXXXI A). The doors in each block were found to be in a strict alignment of each other. The central hall of the central block, measuring 11.50 x 3.42 m., was possibly used as an audience-hall intercommunicating with all the rooms. The rooms may have served as residential block for the ruler.

The last structural Phase, wherein no N.B.P. Ware was recorded, can be dated to *circa* first-second century A.D.

The superstructure in the central and eastern blocks was found to be collapsed. From a study of the remnants, it can be inferred that they formed part of a dome that adorned the building. The entire superstructure in the different blocks and galleries collapsed on a layer of ash, about 5 cm. in thickness, indicating that the palace was destroyed by an extensive conflagration.

There is evidence that the area of the palace was occupied subsequently, although the palace as such had ceased to exist. Excavation brought to light remains of six post-palace Sub-phases, represented by shabby floors and equally poor hearths in the passage of the dome and a number of rooms with a different alignment in the north-east corner of the palace, in the area enclosed formerly by the northern and the western stone boundary-walls. On the evidence of pottery and terracottas this Phase could be dated between *circa* A.D. 300 and 600.

The present author begs the indulgence of the readers for having placed before them such long excerpts, but without these the stand taken by Professor Sharma in respect of the phases of the palace-complex and the bases of his datings thereof would have not been clear. It was also necessary to present the case of Professor Sharma in his own words, rather than in the words of the author, for in the latter case a suspicion could have arisen about whether or not the author has presented faithfully Professor Sharma's viewpoint.

A summarization of Professor Sharma's view would now appear to be permissible. According to his first season's observations, the palace-complex had three phases. In the earliest, the enclosure wall was made of 'random rubble'. The wall of the second phase was constructed with a facing of 'dressed stones', the core however, remaining of rubble. In the third phase, the core was made of bricks, while dressed stone were used for the facing.

As regards the dating, Professor Sharma "observed that the random-rubble walls of the first phase were built prior to the Northern Black Polished Ware". He concluded by saying: "According to the stratigraphic evidence, therefore, the origin of the palace goes back to *circa* 600 B.C., if not earlier. It is, thus, not unlikely that *it was occupied by king Udayana,* the renowned contemporary of Buddha. It seems to have been deserted after the fall of the Mitra dynasty."

After the Second season's work, Professor Sharma made two supplementary observations. He divided the first phase into two sub-phases, viz. I A and I B and, on the basis of the painted and incised pottery associated with the former sub-phase, dated the beginning of the first phase "to *circa* eighth century B.C.". He also made some modifications regarding the last phase of the complex, saying that it "could be dated between *circa* A.D. 300 and 600".

The present author would now like to offer his comments on the various aspects of the issue.

In first place, let it be stated that the 'random-rubble' wall and the 'rubble-core-*cum*-ashlar-facing' wall do *not* represent two different phases. They represent only a single construction, the random-rubble portion representing the foundation part of the total structure of which the rubble-core-*cum*-ashlar-facing portion was what stood above the then ground-level. This fact was clearly discernible in the section of a trench on the northern side of the wall. This had been dug by Professor Sharma himself, but the author took the opportunity to scrape it afresh and re-examine it. In the soil-section against the wall (cf. pl. I) one can clearly see the edge of a narrow, almost vertical foundation-trench going up to the height of the random-rubble portion of the wall. Just where the ashlar facing begins, one may see against it an accumulation of stone-chips representing the building-debris. In the upper part of the section may be seen further chips and stone-rubble, the latter perhaps representing the fall of the structure. It may incidentally be added that this phenomenon of a close-fitting foundation-trench is also to be seen in the section of a trench against the wall, already published by Professor Sharma in *Indian Archaeology 1960-61,* pl. LVIIA.

In this *I.A.*-photograph may also be seen a pit, to the right of the vertical scale. The ground-level at which this pit was dug also seems to have been roughly the level at which the foundation-trench for the palace-wall was excavated.

As may be seen from the photograph (pl.I), the foundation-trench had cut through several occupational layers, and it is these layers that yield the Northern Black Polished Ware, of which many a specimen was collected by the author and the scholars who visited the site along with him. Since Professor Sharma did not take cognizance of the foundation-trench it was but natural for him to think that the random-rubble wall was contemporary with the N.B.P. Ware. Further, since the early levels of the N.B.P. Ware at Kausambi had been assigned by Professor Sharma to *circa* sixth century B.C., it was, again, natural for him to think that the palace belonged to Udayana who did rule at Kausambi most likely about that very time.

Thus, the basic trouble, in a nutshell, arose out of the fact of not having recognized the foundation-trench.

It has been stated by Professor Sharma that some sherds of the N.B.P. Ware, as also Sunga terracottas and a seal, were found further up in the section. Once the phenomenon of the foundation-trench is duly understood and appreciated, the problem of the few N.B.P. Ware sherds and Sunga terracottas occurring further up will also become comprehensible. The palace-wall on the northern side, excluding the corner towers, is about 130 m. in length and about 6 m. in width. The foundation-trench is roughly $1^{1/2}$ m. in depth. Now if about 1200 cubic metres of the strata containing the NBP Ware and Sunga terracottas, etc. had been dug away on the northern side for the foundation-trench, which was not refilled by the same stuff but by rubble stones, where will all this material go? It evidently got spread out alongside the palace-wall and it is because of this that Professor Sharma got the N.B.P. Ware sherds and Sunga material even higher up.

The question that now arises is: if the palace-complex was neither contemporary with the N.B.P. Ware nor with the Sunga terracottas and seals, to which period did it really belong? A thorough examination of the structure itself gave the author the clue.

Embedded in the rubble core of the palace-wall (which had an ashlar veneer) were observed many fragments of architectural stone which had evidently belonged to some earlier structure, were collected there-from and incorporated in the core of the palace-wall. While pl. II A shows the location of one such architectural piece, pl. II B gives its close-up. Plate III A shows another architectural piece found embedded in the core of the wall on the inner side.

In the southern part of the palace-complex (i.e. on the Yamunā side) there is a large-sized habitational building to which Professor Sharma has himself made a detailed reference. Its walls were made of brick bats, amidst which stone-blocks were incorporated here and there. While pl. IV B gives a general view of one such wall, pl. IV A gives a close-up of some of the stones with mouldings.

Within this southern residential complex, there is another architectural piece of great significance (pl. V A): Of stone, it was evidently the capital of some pillar. In fact, it was found close to a doorway and may have belonged to one of its jambs. This capital reminds one of the capitals seen in the Khusro Bagh Gateway-complex at Allahabad (pl. VB). Although the two are not identical, nor does one expect them to be so, the general resemblance does give a rough idea of the approximate chronological horizon of the Kausambi specimen. The Khusro Bagh complex belongs to the early seventeenth century A.D., and the Kausambi capital may not be very far removed from it in time.

Attention in this context may also be drawn to the mason's marks found on some of the stones in the palace-complex. The stone on pl. VI A shows a trident (*trisula*), whereas that on pl. VI B, a 'double-axe' (*damaru*). Though it is not possible to pin-point the chronological horizon of these mason's marks, it is fairly well known that such marks do occur on the structures of the medieval times. Perhaps a closer look even at the Khusro Bagh buildings may reveal identical marks. (Because of lack of time, this was not attempted.)

Here is now some other kind of evidence for consideration. On pl. LXXXII B of *Indian Archaeology 1961-62,* Professor Sharma gives a photograph of incised red ware sherds found associated with Phase I A of the palace-complex. According to him, these potsherds are similar to those found associated with 'post-Harappan chalcolithic sites in western and central India' (*I.A.* 61-62, p.51). It is this pottery that tempted him to push the date of the palace even before the sixth century B.C., viz. "to *circa* eighth century B.C.". For the convenience of the readers, pl. LXXXII B of Professor Sharma is reproduced here as pl. VIIA. Alongside it is pl. VII B which shows the incised red ware found in the medieval levels of Sringaverapura, near Allahabad, currently under excavation. Though no absolute dating evidence by way of an inscription, coins, etc. was found in the strata yielding this incised red ware at Sringaverapura it was duly noted that these strata were much later than those which yielded the coins of the Gahadavala king Govind Chandra (A.D. 1114-55). In any case, the medieval horizon of the Sringaverapura incised red ware is not in doubt. Correspondingly, the Kausambi specimens may also belong to the medieval times.

Juxtaposed to the inner face of the northern peripheral stone-wall of the palace-complex (opposite the place where there is an oblong bastion on the exterior) there is a house-complex. A wall of this complex is seen on pl. VIII A. While behind the person in the photograph (he is Shri Lal Singh of the Excavations Branch of the Archaeological Survey of India), is the boundary wall of the palace-complex, with its rubble-core-*cum*-ashlar-facing, on the left-hand side of the person is a wall of the house under reference. One of the stones *incorporated* in this wall bears an inscription. The stone concerned is to the left of the uppermost white mark of the scale shown on pl. VIII A. Plate VIII B gives a close-up of this inscription. Although the entire inscription is not very clear, at least the first three letters are readable, which are respectively *de va sri.* The reading of the fourth and fifth letters is not so clear. Be that as it may, this inscription is in Devanagari characters which in no case can be earlier than the 12th-13th century A.D. Now, if the stone had originally belonged to another structure from which it was dislodged and incorporated in this palace-complex, the palace-complex would have to be later than the thirteenth century. (How much later, nobody would, of course, be able to say on the basis of this evidence alone.) But if it is argued that the inscription was contemporary with the palace-complex, even then a medieval date is indicated for the complex. It is, however, not unlikely that the defenders of the 'Udayana thesis' may adduce an argument that this slab has been inscribed much later than the construction of the palace-complex, even then how can one run away from the other pieces of evidence adduced in this paper, particularly those relating to the incorporation of moulded or carved stone-pieces within the core of the structure itself (cf. pls. II B, III A, IV A, etc.) or to the occurrence of incised red ware (pl. VII A) which is similar to that found in the late medieval levels of Sringaverapura (pl. VII B).

To sum up, the following facts emerge very clearly:

1. The identification of the foundation-trench (pl.I) shows that the 'random-rubble wall' and the wall with 'rubble-core-*cum*-ashlar-facing' do *not* belong to two phases, but are respectively the below-ground and above-ground parts of one and the same structure.

2. Since the foundation-trench was cut

1. This inscription was spotted by Shri M.N. Deshpande during the joint visit, and the author is greatly beholden to him for it.

through the strata which contained the N.B.P. Ware, Sunga terracottas and even some material ascribable to the early centuries of the Christian era, the palace-wall was decidedly later than these.

3. The incorporation of architectural fragments within the core of the outer stone-wall of the palace-complex (pls.II A, II B and III A) as also in the brick-bat wall (pls.IVA and IVB) of the residential complex on the south, clearly establishes that the palace-complex was later than these architectural pieces.

4. The inscription found on a stone incorporated in the wall of a house in the palace-complex (pls.VIII A and VIII B) is in Devanāgarī script which in no case can be earlier than the 12th-13th century A.D.

5. The stone-capital shown on pl.V A is not much dissimilar to the capitals used in the Khusro Bagh complex (pl. V B) of the early seventeenth century A.D. Though this does not give a precise dating for the Kausambi palace-complex, yet a rough chronological horizon seems to be indicated.

6. The incised pottery (pl. VII A) found associated with Phase I A of the Kausambi palace is similar to that found in the late medieval levels at Srin.gaverapura (pl. VII B).

From all the foregoing facts it is abundantly clear that the palace-complex at Kausambi, which Professor Sharma dated to the sixth century B.C. and thereby associated it with King Udayana, may really belong to a period roughly around the sixteenth century A.D.

EDITORIA ADDITION

The editor, like K.V. Soundara Rajan (*Puratattva* No. 11) fully subscribes to the views put forward by Professor B.B. Lal. After a personal visit to the site along with Mrs. Aruna Tripathi, a Research Scholar in the Ancient History, Culture and Archaeology Deptt. and Sri C.D. Tripathi, Additional Secretary, Union Public Service Commission, who is also a noted historan specializing in the political and cultural history of Assam and close examination of the scrapping of the section cut in the depoit against the Palace wall by Prof. B.B. Lal, Sri M.N. Deshpande and Sri K.N. Dikshit, he too came to the similar conclusions. Additionally, he examined more than 2000 art and architectural fragments kept in bags and marked with all details — trench number, locus, layer, etc. — now housed in the museum attached with the Department of Ancient History, Culture and Archaeology, University of Allahabad. Some of the architectural fragments, which clearly belong to the medieval period, were recovered from these bags. All of them bear markings in black ink which show that they were recovered from the 'Palace-Complex' area. All these pieces were shown to Prof. B.B. Lal at Allahabad and he made some drawings of these works of art and architecture.

I.

II A.

II B.

III A.

III B.

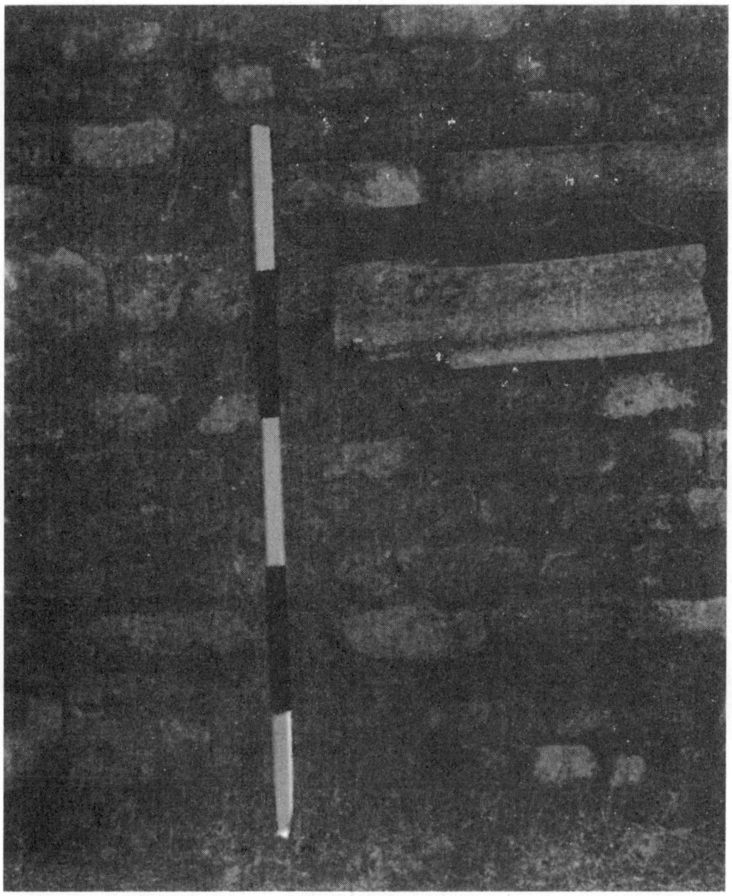

IV A.

IV B.

V A.

V B.

VI A.

VI B.

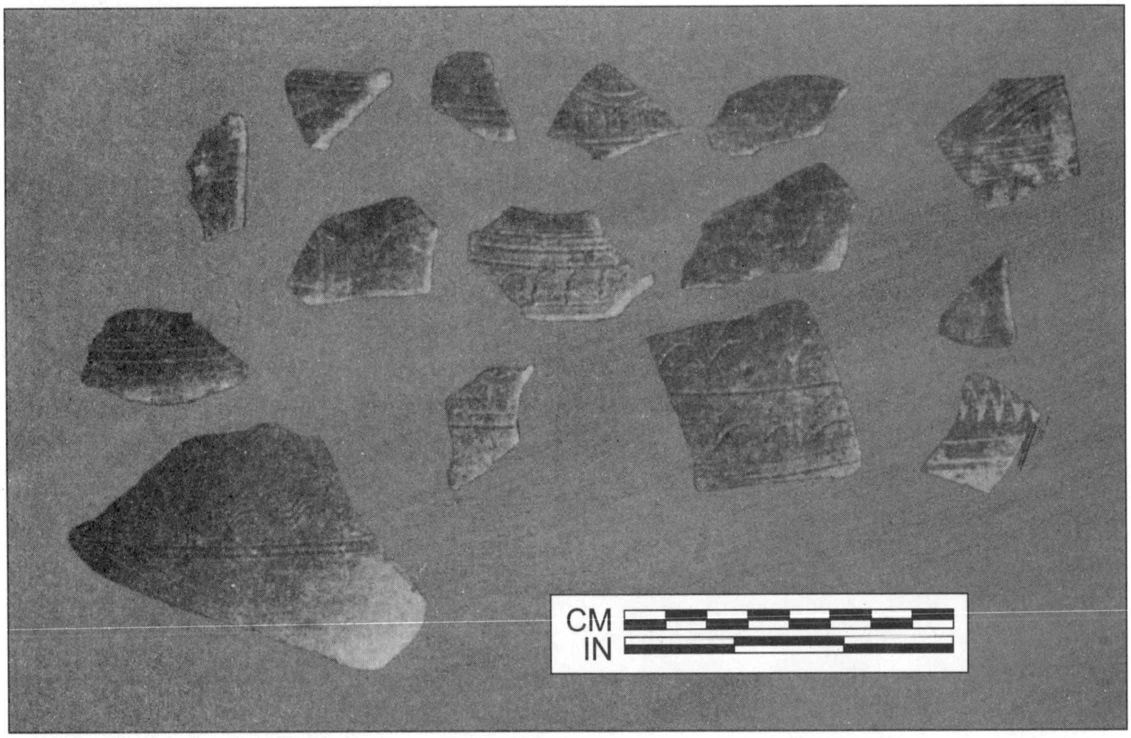

VII A.

VII B.

VIII A.

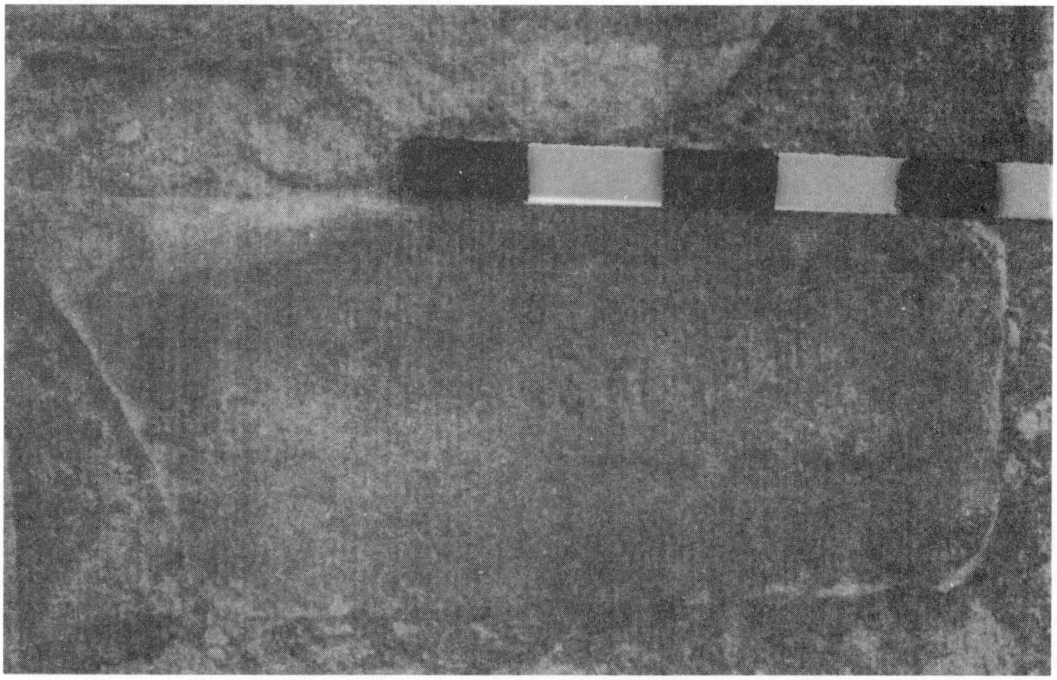

VIII B.

THE SO—CALLED SYENACHITI AT KAUSAMBI : A FALLEN BRICK-MASS

B.B. Lal

While writing a paper on the defences at Kausambi (*Puratattva*, no. 11, 38-95), the present writer had mentioned that he would offer his comments another papaer on the so-called *Syenachiti* (eagle-shaped alter) identified by Professor G.R. Sharma at that site (Sharma 1960, 87 ff.). This, however, could not be done owing to the work on hand relating to the project, Archaeology of the Ramayana Sites'. Meanwhile, many scholars — not only archaeologists but also those dealing with religion and rituals — have made personal enquiries from the writer about his views on the subject. It has, thus, become alsmot incumbent to find time and write out a note, howsoever brief, indicating what the writer thinks of this affair of the *Syenachiti* at Kausambi. This altat is said to have been constructed in connection with a *purusha-medha* (human sacrifice). The writer proposes to deal with the topic essentially from the archaeological angle, leaving the scriptural nuances to specialist in that branch of learning.

LOCATION

As the plan of the area concerned would show (cf. Sharma 1960, fig. 2; relevant portion reproduced here as fig. 1), the location of the so-called *Syenachiti* is immediately outside the defence-wall, in a moat which went round the defences. The line-drawing also shows that the so-called right wing of the eagle actually overrides Revetment 3. The same may be seen in Plate I (same as Sharma 1960, pl.12) (Please see elsewhere below for the real reason of this kind of 'overriding'.) As to the moat, Sharma himself has acknowledged its existence (cf. fig.1). Besides, attention may also be drawn to pl. II (same as Sharma 1960, pl 30 A). In its may be seen the bottom-line of the moat, which was dug into the natural soil, as well as the successive layers of sand and silt which got deposited during the course of time. The evidence of the moat can be seen even further south of the area under discussion. Does one expect the construction of the *syenachiti* - a ritual structure - in a location like this ?

ORIENTATION

Although, as already stated, the present writer has not specialized in the study of ancient rituals, he has nevertheless some elementary idea about them. Take, for example, the question of orientation of various kinds of sacrifical altars. It is enjoined by the ancient texts that the *Ahavaniya* fire is to be on the east of the *Garhapatya* and the main Vedı in between. If there is any further extension beyond the *Ahavaniya,* the same has to be along this west-east axis. [cf. for example, Apte 1926, pp. 1-3, or Ramachandran 1953, pls. I (a) and (b)]. In the case of the *syenachiti* too no exception is to be made. Thus, the figure of the eagle to be portrayed on the horizontal plane of the sacrificial ground has to have its central axis west-east, the head being towards the east and the tail towards the west. In the case of the Kausambi example, on the other hand, the central axis is from north-north-west to south-south-east, the head being towards the latter direction. This is quite contrary to the injunctions of the sacred texts which would have no doubt been followed had this brick-complex been really a sacrificial altar in the fom of a *syenachiti*

We may now offer comments on source of the topics dealing with the constructional aspect of the *syenachiti* and on the objects associated therewith, just to give an idea of the inconsistency that exists between what has been stated by Sharma and the hard reality.

THE PILING OF VEDIKA NO. 4

While referring to Vedika no. 4, Sharma observes (1960, 88):

"The bricks of different shapes and sizes, into which they were *cut before*

> *baking,* were placed inside it _ The bricks are triangular, rectangular, five-sided and six-sided."

Sharma gives a photograph of this 'Vedika' (his Plate 30 B) which is reproduced here as pl.IV B From it one may clearly see that the bricks are all broken, and have acquired their multiple-sided character as a result of this breakage. In order to cross-check my impression gained from the photograph I requested the then Head of the Department, Professor J.S. Negi, kindly to let me have a look at these supposed 'triangular', 'five-sided' and 'six-sided' bricks. He was kind enough to organize it and the bricks concerned were seen by me, along with Professor Negi, as well as Dr. Brij Bhushan Misra and Shri Gupta (Pottry Assistant) of the Department on 29 September 1983. After a careful examination of these bricks, we all agreed that the many-sidedness of the bricks was due to their *breakage,* which was *post-firing. These were not cut before baking* to give them the required shape. The broken edges were rugged and uneven and their outlines were irregular. Had these bricks been made deliberately as 'five-sided', six-sided, etc. the edges concerned would have been smooth and straight.

'SPEICAL BRICKS'

Sharma keeps on stating every now and then in his report that the bricks he is dealing with are 'special'. For example, on p. 125 of his book he states as follows:

> "Other special bricks recovered from the area of the body are --- 1 *Visva-jyotis, 7 Pranabhrts on the frontal range, 2 valakhilyas close to the* row of the *Pranabhrts,* 3 *Chandasyas* along the left fringe and 12 along the right fringe. There are a number of *Lokamprnas* and clod-bricks (*Yajusmatis*) also. *All the special bricks are marked with there lines."* (Italics by the present writer.)

Sharma has not given photographs of these so-called special bricks, which would have made it easier for the present writer to offer his comments. At the same time, it must be stated that all excavators are familiar with the phenomenon that that bricks at most of the early historical sites in the country do bear these "three lines." Some times these are four. These are 'finger-marks' and were produced before the bricks were laid out for drying. These are also known to archaeologists as 'frog-marks', and are thought to have been provided there in order that the mortar may get into them and the bricks may have better cohesion with one another. Anyway, what is more important is that such marks, being a common feature of the bricks found at almost all early historical sites, cannot be taken to make the Kausambi example as 'special bricks'.

THE ASHADHA

Once again while making a reference to some 'notworthy' bricks sharma says (p. 123):

> "The most significant brick, placed at a distance of 1 ft. 9 ins. from the central kankar nodule towards the front, may be identified with the *Asadha* on the basis of its shape, size, line-marks colour, texture and placing. The *Trapezoid* shape, the three line-marks-curved line, straight lines, does, etc. .... all these are in accordance with the rules laid down in the texts in respect of this brick."

Continuing his comments in respect of this bricks, Sharma adds (p. 126):

> "There is sufficient evidence to conclude that this fire-altar (*the syenachiti*) was piled up for the performance of the Purusamedha. On the most prominent brick, Asadha, appears the scene of a human sacrifice --- a man tied to a *Yupa* with a rope and some instrument falling down on his neck."

The brick concerned is reproduced here as pl IV A. It is now for the reader to see for himself/herself *if he/she can make out ' a man tied of a Yupa* with a rope and some instrument falling down on his neck'. To the present writer, however, it would appear that these marks have been created as a result of the burning off (during the process of firing) of the pieces of straw shich had got mixed up with the clay which the brick was under preparation. The marks occur not merely in the lower part of the brick where Sharma sees the scene of man-slaughter, but practically all over the brick: some marks are deep and some others shallow. It may also be noted that the brick had *not been made* trapezoidal in shape. On the other hand, it has acquired that shape because of breakage, the evidence of which is clearly provided by the right-hand and bottom edges. The broken wavy edge at the bottom is far too clear to be missed !

THE UKHA

The *Ukha* is an important vessel associated with the ritual. Sharma has identified it with the pot illustrated here on pl. II and fig. 2 (respectively pl. 32 A and fig. 18, 1 of Sharma's book).

On pp. 148-51 of his book, Sharma gives a very detailed description quoting from the scriptures, of the clay and degraissant to be used for the making of the *Ukha,* as also of its shape, etc. Here one may re-quote that part relating to the shape, which alone (and not the clay-constituents, etc.) the photograph and drawing can illustrate.

> "Sayana gives the following details regarding the shape of the *Ukha,* on the basis of the T.S.B. (*Brahmana* portion of the *Taittiriya Samihita.*). He says that it should consist of three parts so as to look like three pots placed upon one another with a chord round the neck or the junction of the first and second part to represent symbolically the meeting of the three worlds and also to make them firm."

In the foot-notes to the above-quoted sentences, Sharma himself gives the original excerpts from the Vedic texts relating to most of these aspects. For lack of space the same are not given here in detail, but one may still quote Sayana in the original when he explains in detail what the *Ukha* looks like:

> *"Yatha bhandasya = upari = anyad = bhandani, tasya = upari punar = anyad = bhandam = itikakshatrayam, tatha = iyam = eka = eva ukha kakshatraya karya."*

Sharma has laboured hard (pp. 121-22) to convince the reader that the pot illustrated by him conforms to the scriptural description given above. But most of the scholars who have seen the original specimen lodged in the Museum attached to the Department and with whom the present writer had the occasion to discuss the matter do not appear to be convinced of Sharma's identification. To the writer the pot concerned appears to be the broken lower part of a storage jar. It is thick-sectioned, as storage jars usually are, and has a ring-base. Sharma has drawn and photographed the pot upside down (vide his fig. 18, 1 and pl. 32 A). The same are given here as these should be (fig. 2 and pl. II).

IRON MODEL OF A SNAKE

In regard to this Sharma has to say (p. 122):

> "The texts of the Krsna Yajurveda School prescribe that the head of a snake should be placed in the first layer. Here also the iron model of a snake has been discovered in this layer".

For the past five-six years, the present writer has been trying hard to have the *darshna* of this 'iron model of the snake', by writing to and personally requesting Professor Sharma and all his worthy successors as the Head of the Department. Even during his most recent visit to the University, on 12 August 1985, the writer made one more attempt to pursuade the person holding charge of the Kausambi antiquities to let him have a look at this model. But to no avail. Of course, unless the piece is physically examined, nothing final ought to be said in the matter. At the same time, it appeats that the objects in question (fig. 2 here, and fig. 18,4 of Sharma's book) may well be an arrow-head which got bent owing to one reason or another. For example, item 9 of pl.

40 of Sharma's books shows a bent arrow-head, though the bend in this example is near the middle of the tang whereas in Sharma's 'snake' it is nearer the tip. Attention may perhaps be drawn to another example, no. 4, on the same plate, in which there are two bends, one in the tang-part and the other near the tip, the latter incidentally, also giving the impression of a snake-hook.

THE RIGHT WING

We may now turn our attention to some structural components of the *syenachiti*. And we take, as an example, what Sharma calls the 'right wing' of the bird *syena* (eagle). On p. 90 of his book, he observes as follows:

> "The wing, as already pointed out, has three divisions. The outer division joins the body at the shoulder, and at this juction the bricks are placed vertically. In the outer wings, from the shoulders right up to the cross-spine, bricks of natural shape and size are laid own upon one another into courses almost similar to those of a regular structure. The top courses are slightly tilted and disjointed on account of the subsequent robbing of the area. At the point where the cross-spine touches the inner side of the outer wing, there is a complex knob of bricks of which sixteen are intact, and sixteen courses of bricks are visible between this knob and the shoulder joint."

Plate 27A published by Sharma in support of what he has said, is reproduced here as pl. I, in order that the reader may straightaway be able to have a look at it. In this photograph one can easily identify the 'sixteen courses of bricks' referrred to by Sharma in his last sentence. From the photograph it is abundantly clear that this brick-mass represents the fall of the adjacent brick-revetment of the defences. Also, on overall view of the same may be had from pl. III A. The sixteen courses referred to by Sharma and seen in a closer view in pl. III B represent the facing-courses of the revetment, while the higgledy-piggledy bricks to the right of these course belong to the core-part of the revetment. In fact, one may even observe that many of the core-bricks, though dislodged from their original position, are still lying within the frame-work of the revetment.

SO IS IT A SYENACHITI OR A FALLEN BRICK-MASS ?

What has been stated in the preceding paragraph is also fully supported by pl. 28 of Sharma, reproduced here as pl. III A for the ready reference of the reader. In it also may be seen the courses of the brick-facing which have slid down from their original position. On the left of these facing-bricks may also be noted the bricks constituting the core.

A very pertinent question may perhaps be posed now. If this brick-mass does represent a deliberate construction, be it for a *syenachiti* or even something else, how come, that there is not even a single horizontal brick in it ? All the bricks are lying higgledy-piggledy, at all sorts of angles. Again, in a deliberate construction one would expect the bricks to have been laid out at some predetermind level. Nothing of that sort is to be seen in either pl. III A or pl. III B, both giving a close-up of the brick-mass. On the other hand, these photographs show that the bricks are lying on a sharp downward slope near the base part of the revetment. As has already been mentioned in the paragraph dealing with 'location' this brick-mass lies in what was really a moat adjacently outside the revetmet of the defences, and the slope one sees in pl. II against which the fallen bricks lie, is nothing but the edge of this moat. In this context attention may once again be drawn, even at the cost of repetition, to pl. II (same as Sharma's pl. 30A). Herein 'A is the revetment, 'B' the brick fallen from the damaged part of the revetment, 'C' the accumulation of silt, sand and occasionally fallen brick-bats in the moat, and 'D' the natural clay into which the moat was cut. As stated earlier, the photograph also clearly shows the bottom-line of the moat. The few odd bricks that fell on the layers of silt and sand which got accumulated in the moat from time of time, lie horizontally in contrast to the bricks of the revetment which collapsed *en masse*.

Looked at from all the various angles referred to the preceding pages, the so-called *syenachiti* comes out to be nothing but a brick-mass fallen from the revetment of the defences into the adjacent moat.

REFERENCES

1. Apte, R.N. 1926 Some points connected with the Constructive Geometry of the Vedic Altar, *Annals of the Bhandarkar Institute,* vol. VII, pts. I and II, pp. 1-16.

2. Ramachandran, T.N. 1953 Asvamedha Site near Kalsi, *Journal of Oriental Research Madras,* Vol. xxx, pts I-IV, pp. 1-31.

3. Sharma, G.R. 1960 *The Excavations at Kausambi 1957-59,* Allahabad, Department of Ancient History, Culture and Archaeology, University of Allahabad.

Description of Figures and Plates

Fig. 1 Kausambi: Plan showing the location of the *syenachiti vis-a-vis* the defences.

Fig. 2. Kausambi: A, the 'Ukha' as drawn bv Sharma. This is in fact the bottom part of a storage jar and should have been drawn as in B.

Kausambi: C—E, Iron arrow-heads. F, 'an iron model of a snake', according to Sharma.

Pl. 1. Kausambi: The person in the right half of this photograph is brushing revetment (Revetment 3) of the defences. The brick-mass in the foreground is the debris fallen from the revetment whose left-hand half is badly damaged. Sharma calls this fallen debris a *syenachiti* ((eagle-shaped altar) meant for *Purushamedha* (human sacrifice).

Pl. II Kausambi: A, Revetment 3 of the defences; B, the fallen brick-debris; C, layers of silt and sand, with occasional brick-bats, which got accumulated in the moat which was cut into the natural soil (whitish) marked D. One can see the dipping edge and bottom of the moat in the lower part of the photograph:

Pl. III A Kausambi: close-up of a part of Revetment 3 (left) and of the fallen therefrom. The bricks lie in a slope against the edge of the moat which was immediately outside the revetment of the defences. view looking west-north-west.

Pl. III B. Kausambi: another close-up of Revetment 3 (right) and of the bricks fallen therefrom. In this plate as well as in pl. III A one can clearly identify the displaced courses of bricks which originally constituted the facing of the revetment.

Pl. IV A. Kausambi: Accoring to Sharma, 'the *Ashadha* brick showing the scene of a human sacrifice --- a man tied to a Yupa with a rope and some intrument falling down on his neck.

Pl. IV B Kausambi: According to Sharma, 'Vedika 4 Garhapatya'.

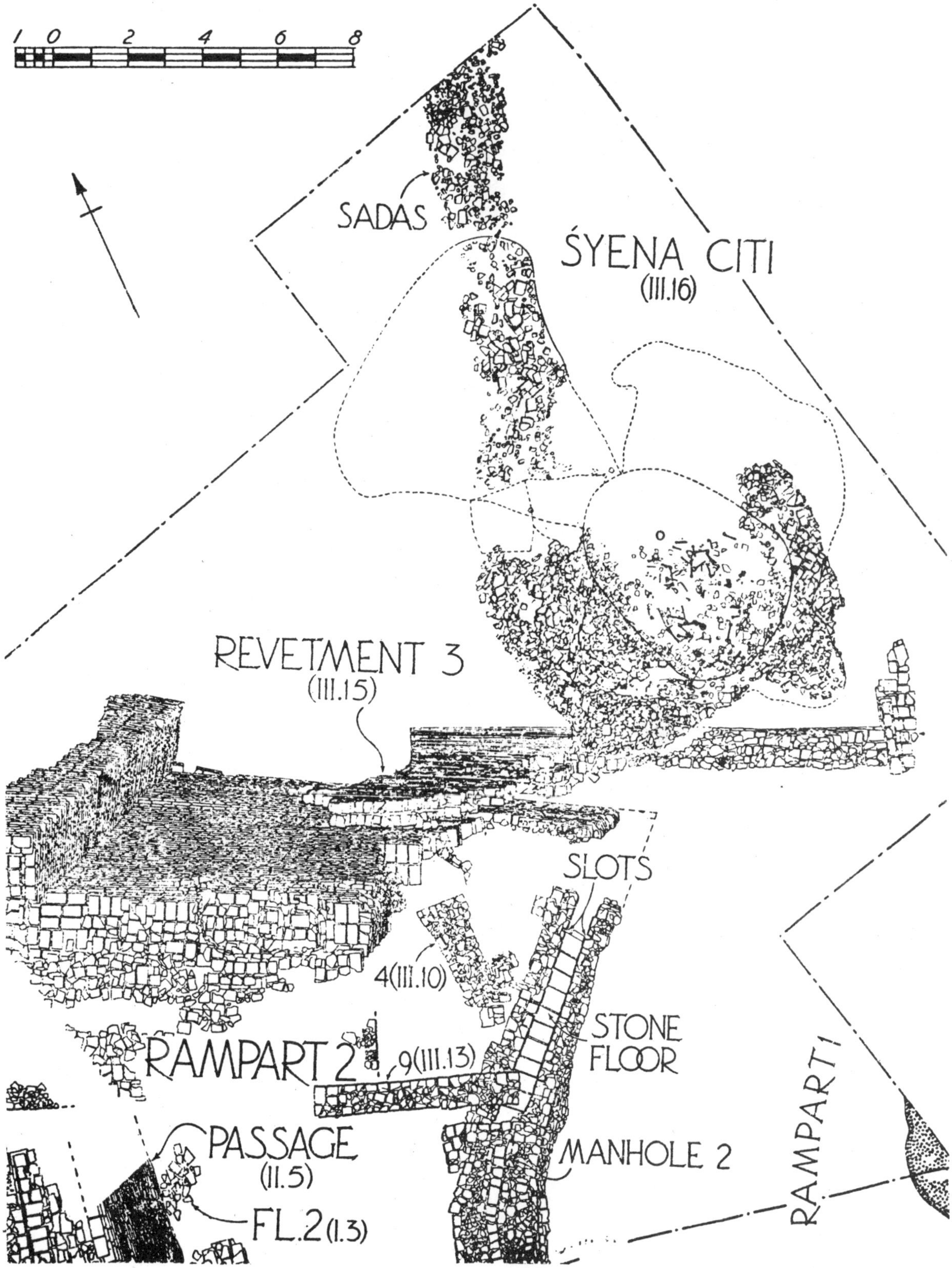

KAUŚĀMBĪ, 1957-59 - PLAN OF THE DEFENCES

Figure 1.

A.

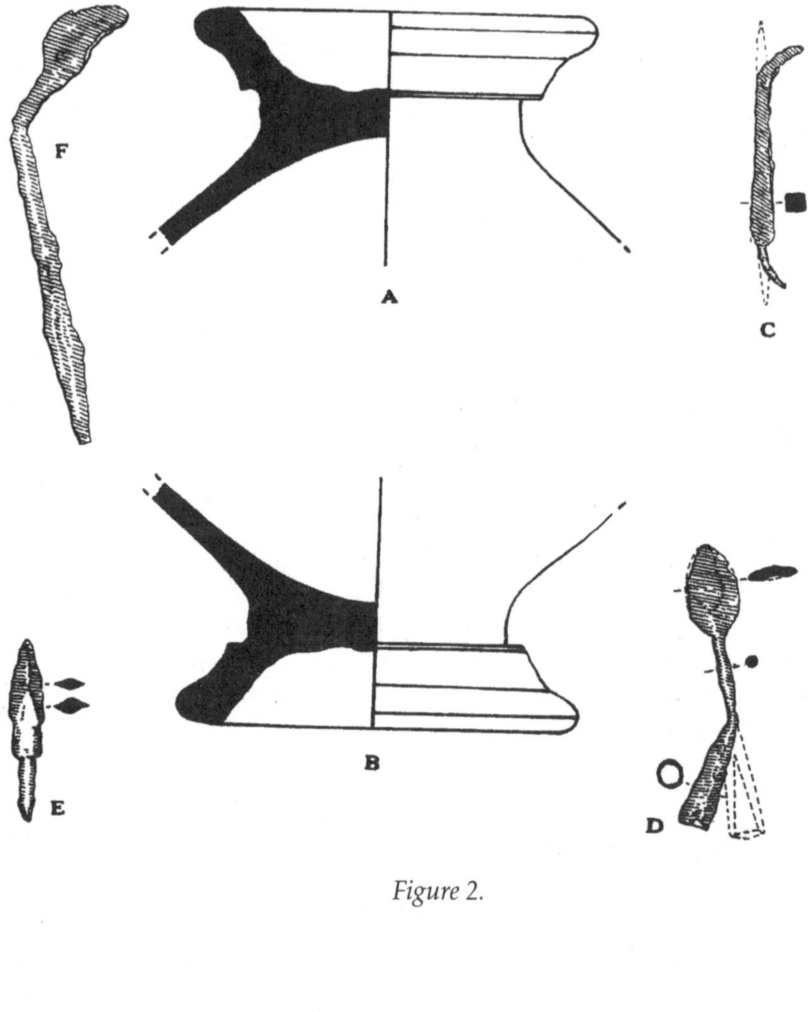

Figure 2.

I.

II.

III A.

III B.

IV A.

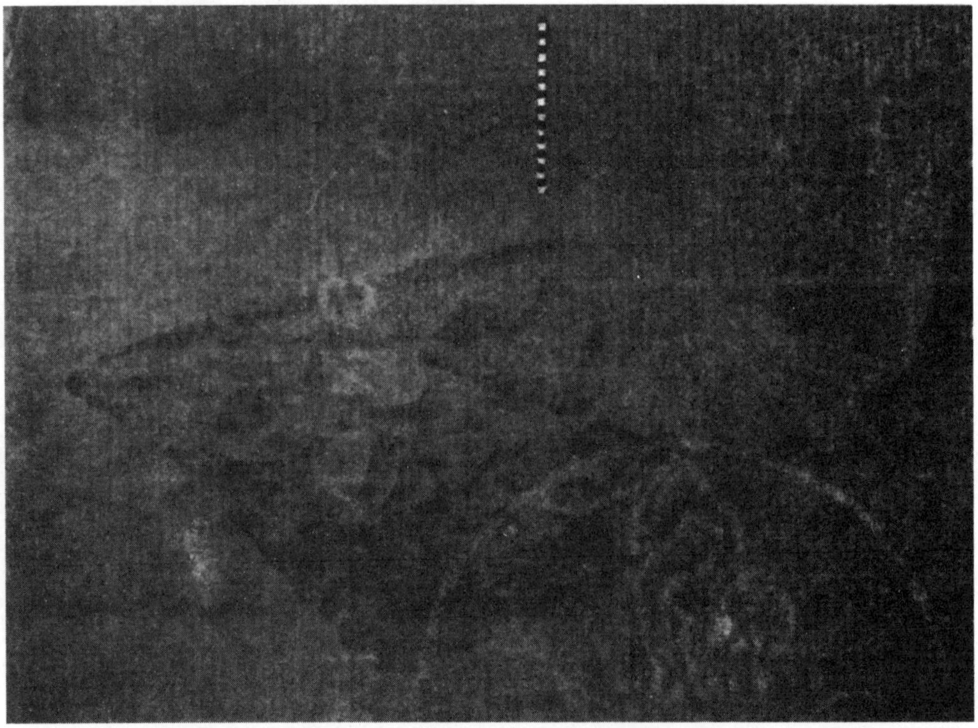

IV B.

GLAZED WARE IN INDIA

K.K. Mohammed

Glazed ware can be defined as that pottery the body of which is coated with a thin layer of film glass to make it insular, impervious and hygenic. Explorations and excavations at a number of sites have yielded a good amount of materials, providing useful informations about the cultural milieu, socio-economic conditions and the advanced pottery technique of the period. But it is unfortunate that neither the published reports have given it the importance it deserved nor a worthwhile study of it has been attempted.

The art of glazing was well known in Egypt even in predynastic period (Furnival: 1904: 34-35). In Nubia, Reisner is said to have found a large number of glazed pottery pieces in a tomb dated to the 12th dynasty (Reisner: 1916: 87 pt 11). The ware appeared about 1000 B.C. in Mesopotamia and was found in abundance at the time of Nebuchadnezzar. The palace of Sargon had its walls decorated with glazed brick (B. Fletcher : 1954:835). The famous tower of Babel at Nimrud had seven stories each of which was decorated by different coloured tiles attributed to the particular planet to which it was dedicated (Furnival: 1904:27). The art of glazing has been reported from Mohenjodaro (Marshall: 1973: 686-87). Excavations at Desalpar has also yielded few sherds of glazed ware (*IAR* : 1963-64:11). Excavations at Shah-ji-ki Dheri near Peshawar has revealed a monastery and a stupa, the construction of which is attributed to Kanishka. It is remarkable that this structure has a Kharoshti inscription with glazing over it (D.B.Spooner: 1908-9:55). A Buddhist shrine excavated near Dal Lake in Srinagar and a courtyard were paved with tiles of different colours. The facade of the shrine was also decorated with tiles to a certain height (J.Ph. Vogel: 1962:62.63). Hieun Tsang saw in the upper country roofs with glazed tiles in brilliant colours (E.B.Havell: 1915:85). Pre-sultanate tiles and pottery were found in Gaur and Pandua in Bengal (Furnival: 72, 73, 74,75) and Brahmanabad (Sindh). But they are different from the blue, diapered and banded tiles and potteries that came to India along with the medieval conquerors.

Some scholars have ascribed the origin of glazed pottery to China ignoring the fact that glazed pottery and bricks were in use in West Asian countries in Protohistoric times. They also did not pay attention to the technique involved in both the potteries; they are entirely different from each other. Chinese pottery is made of vitrified clay of a special kind, whereas the other is made by applying a glass like material to an earthen ware base.

In India glazed ware of the type discussed here came along with the medieval invaders, from West Asia. At Hastinapura it was found in levels contemporary with and posterior to the coins of Balban (1206-87) (B.B. Lal: *A.I.*:1954-55, Nos 10 & 11:71). Excavations at Purana Qila also reported the ware in association with the coins of Balban and Muhammed Tuglak (*IAR* : 1969-70:4). Gifts sent by Alauddin Khilji to Vizir Rashid-Al-Din at Tabriz included many beautiful glazed pottery pieces. All the saucers, flat dishes, sherbet bowls, wine ewers and large dishes were ornamented with seven colours. The wine ewers in Lajvard was ornamented with gold designs (E.G. Browne: 1928: 85 no. 47). The earliest glazed tile decoration in medieval India also goes back to 12th and 13th century. Many tombs in Multan, especially of Yusuf Gardizi (1150 A.D.), Shamsuddin Tabrizi, Bahaul Haque (1226-1280) and Ruknuddin are covered with glazed tiles (Cunningham: 1875: 132-33).

The important centres of the pottery were Peshawar, Lahore, Jalandhar, Sialkot, Delhi,

Jaipur, Ajmer, Bikaner, Multan, Tatta, Halla, Kach, Bombay, Brahmpur, Bulandshahr (Khurja), Rampur, Lucknow, Jabalpur, Allahabad, Mirzapur, Raniganj, Vellore, Coorg, Malabar (Feroke) (Watt: 1902-3:89) and Quilon (Nainar: 1942:206; K.A.N. Shastri: 1939:293-5; Moti Chandra: 1977:203). A number of sites have yielded glazed ware of various types. Most important among them are Fatehpur Sikri, Champaner, Purana Qila, Adilabad, Vijaymandal, Khilokheri, Atranjikhera, Buxar, Nagara, Oriup, Panna, Daulatpur Sanghol, Jahanpana (Delhi), Qila-Rai-Pithora (Delhi), Nevasa, Broach, Jajman, Ropar, Ujjain, Bahal, Pataliputra, Chirand, Kurukshetra, Hoshiarpur, Kaseri, Manwan and a number of sites in various parts of the country. Noteworthy shapes were dishes, bowls, vases, trays, dishes, on stand, *surahis* and storage jars. Important patterns were floral motives, geometrical designs, arabesque, dots, spiral foliage with long coiling leaves, knop and flower patterns and human figures in blue, green, brown, chocolate, yellow, orange, red and brown colours. The depiction of living beings were comparatively much less in Indian glazed pottery. Among the pieces examined by the author only two pieces had living beings painted on them: one showed a woman in long flowing dress and curly hair and the other a crab. Depiction of a bird and a duck head is reported by Wheeler from Charsada (Wheeler: 1962:20).

Glazed pottery can be divided into two categories on the basis of the materials by which it was made. The first group was made of sandy friable materials of whitish colour with very little cohesion. Prof. B.B. Lal feels that it was difficult to manipulate the coarse sandy paste into forms either complicated or of a large dimension (Lal, in *Ancient India:* 108:11 1954-5:71). The body thus made is covered by a thin layer of film glass (glaze), which is a mixture of minerals and chemicals. Medieval Indian potters have used both transparent glazes and opaque glazes to decorate the ware. For opaque glazes, oxides of tin, titanium, zirconium, antimony and zinc are used. Glaze materials can be divided into low, medium and high temperature glazes on the basis of thier melting points. Zinc and antimony are low glazes as they melt at below 1000^0C. Tin, titanium and zirconium oxides are known as high temperature glazes and melt only when they are heated above 1250^0C. Important fluxes used in Indian glazed pottery to help the ingredients to glaze melt are borax, lead oxides, lime and sodapotash.

The first category can again be divided into S' graffito, moulded, monochrome, polychrome and Minai wares. S' graffito is a technique in which a design is engraved on the slip covered surface of the ceramic vessel. Sometimes the decoration is done by the wax resistant process. Wax, which has been thinned by the addition of turpentine is heated slightly and is applied on the pot by a brush. The design the artist has in mind should be scratched deep on this wax covered area. In bisque firing the wax burns off, leaving the hand painted design. Such slip carved ware had a wide distribution all over the Eastern Islamic World. (Pope: 1942:153). The S' graffito technique had its origin in Egypt where such vessels were known from the 7th century A.D. (Arthur Lane: 1937-38:34 pl. 5 no. a). The ware has been reported from various sites of Islamic countries (Geza Fehervari: 1973:62). During the middle ages it was widely used in Spain, Italy and occasionally in France and England (Singer: 1957:303). But the S' graffito wares of the Indian type had their development in Afghanistan. The ware excavated by the French team at Bamiyan and Lashkari Bazar are very important in this respect. It has been suggested that there was an atelier which was destroyed when the Mongols raided Bamiyan in 1221 (J.C. Gardin: 1957:242 pls. 1-4, Nos 1-59). The Lashkari Bazar S' graffito pottery has been ascribed the period between the 11th and early 13th centuries.

The moulded wares were often made in two vertical halves and the decoration and the glaze obliterated down the seam where they joined. The monochrome, pottery has a back ground of a single colour usually yellow, green or celedon and sometimes details in other colours are added. This invarioubly had a crackled surface. Though the attempt of the potter was to imitate the celadon ware of China, it did not succeed. Few monochrome pieces, excavated at Fatehpur Sikri by R.C. Gaur and the author, are made of white sandy materials, with a thin glossy glaze. The excavation at Atranjikhera has also yielded such monochrome ware in good numbers. The potters at Quilon in Kerala had mastered the technique of Chinese monochrome ware so well that their monochrome pieces were sold in West Asian countries as Chinese ware (Nainar : 1942:208; K.A.N. Shastri: 1939:293-5). The attempt to use glazes of different colours side by side in the ornament of a single vessel resulted in the production of polychrome ware. The designs were carved in a kind of cloisonne manner, with grooved or raised outlines to segregate the coloured glazes in their appropriate areas. Polychrome was known in Persia as Lakabi ware and Kashan was one of the centres famous for its production. Such polychrome wares have been excavated from a number of places in India.

It is to be noted that the technique employed in all these decorations was underglazing. No piece with overglaze technique was encountered in Hastinapura, Purana Qila, Fatehpur Sikri and Atranjikhera. By 12th century the West Asian potters had developed the technique of over glazing in which the pottery was fired twice, the latter firing being carried out after painting at a low temperature. In underglaze method the piece had to be fired only once at a high temperature in order to fuse the glaze on the vessel and this high temperature destroyed the colour effects of many low temperature colours. As this disadvantage was removed in overglaze method, pottery with varigated colours could be produced. Rayy and Kashan were the famous centres where such pottery was made. Popularly known as Minai or Lajvardina wares this was decorated with an astonishing variety of figures like Chinese lotus, phoenix and dragon. It has close affinity with the art of miniature paintings and the scenes depicted in them. Its presence in India is attested by the fact that the list of gifts sent by Alauddin Khilji to Rashuddin included many Lajvard pieces (E.G. Brown: 1928:85, no.47). In Iraq, Syria and Egypt the technique was completely unknown. Aslanapa is of the opinion that the ware had its origin in Iran and then passed into Anatolia with Seljukes (Aslanapa in *Archaeology,* June 1971:212). But it was little suited to rough use and its surface easily got soiled and defaced. Moreover firing the pot twice also consumed much time. This was exactly the reason why it was considered a luxury item.

Glazed pottery made in Sindh were in two or three shades. If the ground was pale blue, the patterns were made in slightly darker shades of the same colour and designs were made in brown colours if the ground was yellow. Usually floral ornamentations were assorted within panels or medallions, the flowers being in a lighter shade than the ground colour. In Multan pottery, the pattern is first painted with a white slip and then the colour follows. This raises it slightly above the level of the field (Watt: 1903:92). Commonly known as slip technique (raising the painting above the field) this had its origin in 10th century at Afrasiyab and Nishapur in Iran (Katherina in *Islamic Art*: 1973:14-15). Occasionally birds are shown in this ware; then they look like stylized calligraphic emblems. Human forms are never found. It is remarkable that Sindh and Khurja potteries share these characteristics with the Afrasiyab pottery. Delhi and Jaipur pottery are not made out of clay but of ground felspar (burbura) mixed with gum or starch. It cannot be formed on potter's wheel, but moulded or wielded by hand. It is very similar to Martaban wares of Pegu not only in shape but also in materials (Watt: 1903:90). Jaipur pottery has two shades of blue, cobalt and turquoise on a very pure opaque white (Watt: 1903:91). In Khurja pottery also the pattern is raised by the use of slips into slight relief. The pattern consists of a warm orange brown or pale claret coloured field with slightly darker floral designs picked out in white and blue (Watt: 1903:93). Rampur is famous for its deep green-blue *surahis* in one uniform colour, bereft of any pattern on them. It also produces *surahis* in two shades of green and blue with patterns distinctly moulded on the surface (Watt : 1903:93). Peshawar pottery resembles majolica. Its reddish earth body is coated with a dressing of white earth mixed with Kharia *mitti* or chalk obtained from Khaibar. It is then dipped into the glaze of which the base is lead oxide. For ordinary greenish white pottery, nothing else is needed. The design is outlined on the unburnt glaze with manganese oxide and the details are filled with copper oxide and when burnt green leaves outlined in brown are produced on white body. The pottery is often made in green and pink on a milky white, but in the earlier work patches of colours were assorted so as to give the effect of bunches of flowers (Watt : 1903:88-89). Vellore pottery is made from fine clay, which could be subjected to the most delicate treatment on the wheel. It is glazed either emerald green or deep dull brown. The ornamentation is chiefly dog-tooth and stamping different patterns on the plastic materials. The black glazed pottery made at Quilon in Kerala was greately admired by foreign travellers like Yaqut (Nainar:1942:206) Qazvini (Nainar : 1942:208). Muhalhil (Motichandra : 1977:203) and Friar odoric (K.A.N. Shastri: 1939:293-5).

The second category has normal pottery fabric, red medium core and crackled glazed surface. Painting is mostly done on a white slip below the glaze. After being treated with this thick white slip it was dipped into coloured glaze and fired for the second time. The finished pottery has red medium core. Where the glaze lies directly over this core its colour becomes dark, but where the glaze overlies the slip its colour turns pale. Pottery pieces with glazing directly over the red core without the slip has also been reported abundantly. The writer has come across a number of such pottery from Fatehpur Sikri and Atranjikhera. External surface of this type was often undecorated. Excavation at Iznik in Turkey has yielded such wares in profusion (Aslanapa in *Archaeology :* 1971:214). In Turkey it is known as Miletus ware and has stylistic affinities with the peasant wares of Perisa and the coarse Syrian and Egyptian wares of Fifteenth century (Arthur Lane:1957: 41).

The technique of pottery making has been explained in various ways by different authors. Of all the treatises on this subject the most reliable is written by Abul Qasim Kashan on the technique of glazed pottery available in the Constantinople library. He says that glaze is made out of powdered quartz and potash melted together in equal quantities and mixed with water. The body material was composed of powdered quartz, glaze and plastic clay in 10:1:1 (A. Lane:1950:32). The great advantage of this technique was that the glaze and body being mainly composed of the same substance fused inseperably together and couldn't flake apart in the same way as the lead fluxed tin glaze ware. The monograph written by Ustad Ali Mohammed of Tehran on the preparation of glaze is also more or less the same. He suggests the use of Shura-i-brabani, Serg-i-Chekhmaq and Senj-i-Shahdanej for the preparation of the glaze (Furnival: 1904:215-223). After an extensive tour and painstaking survey, the real process involved by potters in India has been dealt with by Birdwood in his *Industrial Arts of India*. The report of Dr. Centre, the chemical examiner about glazed tiles is very helpful in understanding the composition in glazed pottery and the preparation of glaze. His analysis has proved that glaze can be made by melting powdered silicious sandstone with carbonate of soda and mixing the two with metalic oxides to produce glazes of various colours. The body is made by silicious sand, lime and glass and the three ground and made into a paste with rice water. It is then dried at a gentle heat and covered with ashtar, the whole is then dipped in the glaze and placed in the furnace (Vogel:1920:59-60). The account given by Burton Page is not much different from Dr. Centre in substance.

Though the ware has been extensively used in India during the medieval period and a large number of buildings have been beautified by glazed tile covering, it is intriguing that no excavations have unearthed a factory or kiln where the pottery was made. The reason perhaps can be attributed to the very few number of excavations carried out in Medieval sites. Contemporary Indian and Persian sources do not throw any light upon its production, technique, distribution and use. Foreign travellers like Tavernier who have given us graphic discription about Persian glazed ware do not give us any useful information about Indian glazed ware. This has lead Percy Brown to think that glazed tiles were not produced in India but it was imported from Persia. But the fact that there are many distinctly Hindu pictures on many tiles at Gwalior Fort, militates against this view. Excavations have been undertaken at a very few medieval sites. Wherever it was carried out, it was confined to palaces and mansions of nobility. If a proper excavation is conducted at a site, which has a tradition of producing pottery, like Khurja, Peshawar and Bahmanabad, one is bound to come across a factory.

NOTES

1. Yaqut "Vases are made in Kulam (Quilon) and sold in our countries as Chinese vases, but they are not Chinese for the Chinese clay is harder than that and more fire resisting. The clay in this town from which they make vases resembles the Chinese clay. It is left in the fire for three days and cannot be baked any longer. Kulam pottery is black in colour, but that which comes from China is white and of other colours, either translucent or not. It is manufactured in Persia from pebbles and qalai lime, and glass which is smashed up into a paste and blown and worked with pincers giving it the shape of drinking-cups and other shapes. Qazvini repeats the first point mentioned by Yaqut and concludes with the remark that Kulam vases are black in colour, while those of China are white and of other colours." (Nainar:1942:206).

REFERENCES

1. Furnival, 1904 *Leadless Decorative Tiles, Faience and Mosaic,* Staffordshire.

2. Reisner, 1916 *Ancient Egypt,* London.

3. Banistor Ftecher, 1961 *A History of Architecture on the Comparative Method,* London.

4. Marshall, 1973 *Mohenjo-Daro and Indus Civilization,* vol. II, New Delhi.

5. *Indian Archaeology Review,* 1963-64, Delhi.

6. D.B. Spooner, 1908-09 *ASI Annual Report.*

7. E.B. Havell, 1915 *The Ancient and Medieval Architecture of India,* London.

8. J.Ph. Vogel, 1962 *The Goose in Indian Literature and Art,* Leiden.

9. B.B. Lal, 1954-55 *Ancient India,* Nos. 10 & 11.

10. E.G. Browne, 1928 *A Literary History of Persia,* vol. 3 Cambridge, No. 47.

11. Cunningham, 1875 *ASI Annual Report,* 1872-73, Calcutta.

12. Watt, 1902 *Indian Art at Delhi,* Calcutta.

13. Nainar, 1942 *Arab Geographers knowledge of South India,* Madras.

14. K.A.N. Shastri, 1939 *Foreign Notices of South India,* Madras.

15. Moti Chandra, 1977 *Trade and Trade Routes in Ancient India,* New Delhi.

16. Wheeler, 1962 *Charsada, A Metropolis of North-West,* London.

17. Pope, 1942 *The Survey of Persian Art and its cities* London.

18. A. Lane, 1937-38 The Early S' graffito wares of the Near East in *Transactions of Oriental Ceramic Society,* Vol. 15.

19. Geza Fehervari, 1973 *Islamic Pottery, A Comprehensive Study based on the Barlow Collection,* London.

20. J.C. Gardin (1957) Poteries de Bamiyan

in *Ars Orientalis,* vol. II. Paris.

21. J.C. Gardin, 1963 *Lashkari Bazar Ceramiques et Mannaies,* Paris.

22. Katherina, 1973 *The Art of Ceramics in Islamic Art,* Los Angles.

23. Aslanapa, 1971 Turkish Ceramic Art, *Archaeology.* vol. 24 New York.

24. Arthur Lane, 1957 *Late Islamic Pottery,* New York.

25 Singer, 1957 *History of Technology,* vol. II, Oxford.

26. Arthur Lane, 1950 *Early Islamic Pattery,* London.

Salvage Archaeology — Ahmadabad : 1984

R.N. Mehta and Rasesh Jamindar

The stratigraphic development of an active urban settlement could be effectively understood by Salvage Archaeology. It was used effectively for understanding the stratigraphy of Vadodara.

It was thought to apply this too while studying the antiquity and history of Ahmadabad from the view point of toponymy, archaeology and literary references. As Ahmadabad is an active growing metropolis, the only systematic excavation in this city was conducted in the Calico Mill compound.

Such rare opportunities are often not available, so one has to rely on field observations of numerous diggings that are undertaken by private and public undertakings. Fortunately in 1984, specially after the month of September, and in 1985 upto the month of February, the Ahmadabad Municipal corporation was laying some pipelines. The narrow long slits opened in this work reached a depth of about 2.5 metres. These provided some useful data, when they were cutting across the older stratigraphy in the Bhadra and Jamalpur areas. These were carefully surveyed.

Moreover, a large complex of Visala was being developed on the Relief Road in an area, locally known as Sadargehan-no-chaklo. The effort to build undergorund structure led to the digging, reaching upto 5 metres; about seven metres in some selected parts.

These diggings supplied very significant data that throw light on the history of Ahmadabad and its outer fortifications. It may be pointed out that the stratigraphic observations were taken, and the sections examined. However, the minor antiquities created their own problems. Some of them were picked up from the sides of the cuttings. They were good indicators of the location, but others were collected from the dump of the diggings. While collecting them, enquiries were made of their locations in relation to the depth of the excavation and actual observations of the materials; their environmental conditions gave further indication of their strata. These are rather weak tools, but they are better when none other are available.

The work done earlier at Vadodara, Champaner and Khambhat Nagara had given enough background for understanding this period.

2

One of the most important cuttings was on the Relief Road, on the east of Jyotisangh, here a complex of Visala was to be built. Below the present day tar road, the cuttings revealed a phase of brick walls with mud cement. This road was planned in the thirties of the present century. The brick structures, therefore, stratigraphically pointed to an earlier period. Taking the average life of such a brick structure as about a century and a half, they could be placed in the late 18th/ 19th centuries A.D.

They were overlying a large complex of lime and brick structure, with its underground storage tank, etc. This large prosperous structure, stratigraphically pointed to a period earlier than late 18th century. Its fine material would have given it more longivity and, therefore, its beginning could be easily ascribed to the period of early 17th century.

A brick structure was overlying a deposit of about two metres of archaeological debris that was deposited on natural soil. This deposit could fortunately be dated by a copper coin of Mahmud Begada (1458-1511 A.D.), obtained from the section of the cutting from the depth of about 5 metres.

Below the stratum of the coin, there was very thin deposit, suggesting that the incipient activities could be dated to the 15th century. Interestingly, some refuge pits dug from almost this level showed large quantities of bones with cut-marks and burning marks. These bones suggested that the animals were consumed possibly in some feast and were dumped in the refuge pits. Such refuge pits are found in open areas near habitations. Thus, the stratigraphy ranged from the 15th century A.D. to the present day.

As noted earlier, the collection of minor antiquities presented some problems. Those that were taken out form well observed section were the coin of Mahmud Begda, large glazed bowls and a stem of a drinking cup. The other glazed wares and unglazed pottery, were collected as stray finds. They were plain and burnished red wares, plain and burnished black wares, glazed wares of different types and Chinese blue-on-white Ming ware.

These antiquities suggest a date later than 14th century on the basis of similar finds from Calico Mill Compound, Champaner, Vadodara, and Khambhat (Cambay). These indications, both from the stratigraphy and antiquities, throw interesting light on the growth pattern of Ahmadabad.

3

It is generally believed that Ahmadabad was developed by Ahmed Shah in the 15th century A.D. However, the archaeological and literary evidences indicate that Ahmed Shah came to a large township that was already existing, and built his royal residence in the open area near this town of Asawal. The development of the place after this activity of building the palace is known as Ahmadabad.

From the archaeological view point, the areas around Astodia, Sarangpur, Bhanderipura were inhabited but the other part started developing slowly around the palace complex of Bhadra.

In this growth pattern, the observations on Visala has thrown considerable light. The stratigraphy of this site which is within a kilometer to the east of the Laldarwaza indicates that it was on open area with no tracess of habitation prior to the 15th century A.D. In the early part of this century also, there was sparse population and its occasional revelry of feasts is recorded in the refuge pits from this site.

The name of Sadarjehan of this part of the town suggests that the government officials of the rank of Kazi lived in this thinly populated area, near the present day site of Pir Mohammadshah library. The records of *Mirat-i-Ahmedi* notes that the Kazi was active in the 15th century. The archaeological data support the notion of the existence of habitation in this area, but is silent about its name.

Explorations of the topographic features of this area as well as the population pattern seem to support the notions developed by archaeological data. To the north and north-east of this place are the areas of *Habsis* and *Panjarapol*. These features suggest that the occupation of the *Habsis*, who were fairly active in Gujarat court in the 16th century, might have been begun a little earlier in the open area. The *Panjrapol*, also as an institution, indicates the outsirt of a habitation where such activities could be undertaken.

All these features suggest the growth of the city in the 15th/16th centuries A.D. and shed interesting light on the observations of Abul Fazl and Mirza Mohammad Ali Khan. Both these Persian scholars state that Ahmadabad had thrown a number of suburbs around it. This number has been given as 360. It is a traditional figure, signifying the growth pattern of Ahmadabad.

A perusal of the place-names of Ahmadabad supports the statements of these scholars. Around the nucleus of the Royal Palace, a ring of suburbs could be observed. It is interesting that in this ring some older independent habitiation centres were converted into suburbs as well as the development of new suburbs.

A perusal of this suburban development suggests that they usually occupy different areas, leaving open space between them. Eventually, this place gets covered up by the growth of the habitat. The archaeological observations and analysis of other data suggested this type of growth pattern of Ahmadabad, and raised another problem about its outer fort-line.

4

Ahmadabad like Surat had two forts. One of them was the Royal enclosure and the other was an outer fort. The outer fort of Surat was constructed in 1664 A.D. The first fort at Surat was constructed in the Mid-16th century and the outer ring was constructed in the late 17th century. The later construction at Surat was covering a number of suburbs. At Ahmadabad also the situation was analogous and, hence, the construction of this fort-line required some archaeological work.

The outer fort-line was ascribed to Mahmud Begada as stated by Farishta, an author of the 17th century. This view is, however, contradicted and Ahmed Shah is given the credit of this construction.

However, the placement of some monuments like the mausoleum of Ravi Sipri, the *Kachni Masjid,* etc. in the maidan-e-vad, and even Haibatkhan's mosque, the partial covering of some *puras,* and the records of the struggle of Gujarat Sultan Muzaffar III in 1583 A.D. were creating problems in accepting the literary evidence. Therefore, archaeological exploration and salvage archaeology were necessary for solving these problems. It had to be examined from two points: one of them was the examination of the standing parts of the Fort and other was the stratigraphy.

The survey of the standing part of the fort in the Bhadra area suggested that the lower parts on the Sabarmati side had stones with mason marks of about 15th century and earlier periods. This line terminated near *Manek burj.* However, the upper parts were a later addition. The *Ganesha bari,* the *Manek burj,* the wall running from *Manek burj* towards the Mosque of Ahmed Shah did not bear any marks of the earlier construction. On the contrary, this wall had an aqueduct or water chanel running on its top. Its alignment towards the Sarai of Azamkhan clearly suggested that this channel carried water, of either Sabarmati or a well dug in its bed, to the Sarai, and possibly acted as the head for the *Karanj.* Its bricks of the size well-known in the 17th century were also late introduction in Ahmadabad. They were possibly introduced in the 16th century and became popular in the 17th-18th centuries A.D.

Here, these features indicated the new use of the burj, and reminds one of similar features from Champaner, Agra and other sites. It is, therefore, clear that the older *burj* was reused for a different funcion in the 17th century. A further examination of this broken wall near Ahmed Shah's mosque indicated that the complete wall from the core to the outer side was built in one period and, therefore, its superposition on the older wall could not be established on the surface.

The brick construction in the Jamalpur, Khanpur areas also indicated these features and hence it was obvious that the construction cannot be ascribed to the Sultans. The examination of the cross-sections of the fort-line near the gateways also confirmed these observations. Specially the collapse of the side wall in the heavy rains in 1931 indicated that the fort-line had its core of bricks of old and new sizes and it had used mud mortar.

These features not only indicated that the fort-wall was not built in the 15th century; it was a later work. Significantly, these characteristics of construction was observed at Cambay. Here the fort was constructed during the reign of Akbar, after the conquest of Gujarat.

These archaeological observations were pointing to the conclusion that reliance on Farishta for fixing the date of the construction of the fort rests on very weak foundations. Probably, the prestige of Mahmud Begda as a great patron of building activity was responsible for the idea expressed by Farishta.

Fortunately, this opportunity was available as the Municipal Corporation was laying pipe lines. Even though its major work was over, this work was going on in Raikhad and the Jamalpur area.

In the Jamalpur area, diggings between the Khan-jahan-darwaja and Jamalpur-darwaja proved to be of utmost importance. These diggings were done along the wall as well as across the fort-line. These gave excellent opportunity to study the stratigraphy.

The diggings were reaching a depth of about 2.5 m. Two of them were running parallel to the wall, so parts of the fort-wall and parts of the area near the wall were exposed to view. The other cutting was across the wall. All the three cuttings revealed the stratigraphic position of the fort.

It was observed that the foundations of the wall reached to a depth of about 0.75 to one metre. Below this depth there was archaeological debris, and the natural earth. The archaeological debris at different points gave different pictures in the general framework.

At one place, the fort-wall was superimposed on archaeological debris in which were no structural remains. At other places the wall rested, on earlier structure that ran across the wall. This earlier structure of 15th and 16th centuries A.D. was underlying the fortline, and hence it clearly indicated the relative position of this fort-line.

The cutting across the fort-line also showed archaeological debris below it. Thus the structural phase of the fort-line indicated its position, as a superimposed construction on the earlier strata.

These definite stratigraphical observations confirmed the doubts raised by the arrangement of monuments, as well as the analysis of the standing parts of the fort-line. These activities, therefore, suggest that the outer fort-line of Ahmadabad was neither the work of Sultan Ahmad, the builder of Ahmadabad, nor of Mahmud Begda, the famous Sultan of Gujarat; it is the work of Akbar after his conquest of Ahmadabad.

It is a well documented fact that Akbar had to come to Ahmadabad twice in 1572-73, but his rule was opposed by the last Sultan of Gujarat who reconquered Ahmadabad in 1583 A.D. His efforts to reconquer Gujarat Kingdom did not succeed due to the military action taken by Akbar's commanders. But this volatile situation might have been responsible for strengthening the old and building the new fortifications of the city, possibly after 1583 A.D.

These efforts in Salvage Archaeology suggest the following conclusions:

(1) Sultan Ahmad had occupied the area of present day Bhadra.

(2) Parts of the old fort of Bhadra are preserved on the Sabarmati.

(3) The Manek-Burj had changed its function and became a place to draw-water and supply it to Azamkhan's Sarai and possibly Karanj.

(4) The outer fort line of Ahmadabad was built, after its conquest by Akbar.

(5) After the Royal enclosure of Ahmadabad was built, the area towards the east was developing by stages.

(6) There were many open areas in the city and they were slowly occupied.

(7) Except for standing monuments, much of the older works of Ahmadabad lie buried under the present land surface.

(8) Some remains of the older period exist in different parts of the city. These are being examined by Gujarat Vidyapith.

(9) The city of Ahmadabad shows a growth pattern around the nucleus of Bhadra, and on this growth old independent habitations became its suburbs; new suburbs also developed.

(10) Some of these suburbs were included in the fortifications built by Akbar.

(11) The view expressed by Abul Fazl and Mirza Muhammad Ali Khan about the pattern of habitation of the city are generally correct.

(12) Other explorations have indicated the correctness of the *tirthas* of Padma Purana.

(13) For the study of Ahmadabad prior to 15th century A.D. only Salvage archaeology and explorations are effective tools, as literery evidence are vague and require verification by Archaeology.

(14) Further work in this direction is essential not only for Ahmadabad but for all our habitations including Agra, Delhi and other metropoliton centres.

NOTES AND NEWS

Excavations at Hatikara: a Chalcolithic site in West Bengal

N.C. Ghosh and S. Nag

The Department of Ancient Indian History, Culture & Archaeology, Visva Bharati, carried out an excavation at Hatikara. The objectives of the excavations were i) to ascertain the cultural sequence, ii) to find out the spread of the settlement of each of the phases, and iii) to cross-check the evidence revealed by previous excavations at similar other sites in the region.

The site (Lat. $23^0 49^0$;Long. 87^0 35'), is located on the right bank of River Bakreswar, 24 km. north-north-west of Bolpur. At the top, the surface measures 170 m. north-south and 150 m. east-west. The maximum height of the mound from the river level is 6.5 m. A large part of it has been completely eroded and a considerable portion of the remaining part is occupied by the villagers. The area under excavation was thus extremely limited. However, the excavation exposed a 2.55 m. thick habitational deposit of continuous occupation from the Chalcolithic to the Iron Age. It has two main periods of occupation.

Period I (Chalcolithic) is characterised by the occurrence of Black-and-Red Ware, both plain and painted, the type fossil of eastern Indian Chalcolithic. It has a deposit of 1.30 m. at its maximum, and is largely undisturbed. A mud floor, with post-holes and clear indication of two building phases, have been found. Apart from B-and-R Ware, there are black, buff and red wares; the shapes represented are vessels with out-turned rims, jars, bowls, etc. The paintings are usually executed in white on black surface. The animals represented through lines are *Bos indicus* Linn., *Bubalus bubalis* Linn., *Sus scrofa cristatus* Wagner, etc. Microliths and copper objects are conspicuous by their absence. Among other antiquities, mention may be made of a large terracotta double convex disc decorated with notched design, terracotta beads, hospscotch, spindle whorl, stone pestles, etc.

Period II (Iron Age): Apart from iron, this period is associated with a few new wares such as black slipped ware and fine grey ware. There is no hiatus between Periods I and II. The occupation during Period II extended much more than that of Period I. Two floor-levels have been encountered. The earlier one is more compact in nature, made of reddish clay with a hearth on it. Structural layout can be reconstructed from the positions of post-holes on both of them. Several half-burnt mud chunks with impressions of bamboo and reed have been found. The ceramic variety ranges from fine lustrous red ware to coarse gritty ware. The shapes are large jars, bowls, basins, shallow dishes, miniature pots, etc. Among other antiquities mention should be made of beads of semi-precious stones, iron objects, including a crude dagger, clay chunks having impressions of rice and husk. The animals represented are *Bos* sp., *Bubalus bubalis* Linn, *Capra hircus aegagrus* Erxl., besides *Chitra indica* gray. The deposition of the latter part of this period has been disturbed by several pits and signs of conflagration are evident.

Secretary (Protohistory)

Prof. R.C. Gaur

Prof. V.N. Misra

Deccan College

Excavations At Narhan 1983-85

Purushottam Singh, Makkhan Lal and Ashok Kumar Singh

Narhan (Lat. 26°19'N; Long 83°24'E) is located on the left bank of river Ghaghara in Bansgaon Tehsil of district Gorakhpur. There are two mounds at the site.

Our limited sampling of both mounds has brought to light a five-fold culture-sequence ranging in date from middle of the second millennium B.C. to the seventh century A.D. Details regarding each period are as follows:—

Period I: Represented by an average deposit of 1 m on Mound-1 is marked by the occurrence of white painted black-and-red ware, black-slipped ware with occasional paintings in white, red slipped ware and plain red ware. The principal pottery types in black-and-red ware are bowls, basins and vases. Dishes are conspicuous by their absence in this ware. More than 20% sherds in the fine and medium fabrics of this ware are painted.

The first settlers lived in wattle-and-daub houses. Remains of post-holes and reed marks in burnt clay lumps have been found. Mention may be made of a curious looking hearth, partly excavated in Tr. 7. Although the first settlers practised agriculture, meat was an important component of their diet as is evidenced from the presence of charred animal bones; some of them having cut marks. Bones, of humped Indian cattle (*Bos indicus* L.), sheep goat (*Ovis/Capra*), remains of a wild runimant like deer or antelope (? *Axis* sp.) and horse (*Equus sp.*) have been identified in the limited collection of bones studied so far. The small finds include pottery discs in large numbers. Of these, four pieces are perforated and might have been used as toy-cart wheels. Bone points account for 15 pieces and nine terracotta dabbers and two balls, one each of terracotta and stone. No evidence of any metal has been reported so far from the limited dig.

Period II: Represented by an average deposit of 90 cm on Mound-1 is marked by total absence of black-and-red ware, either plain or painted, but the frequency of black slipped ware increases in this period. Although red slipped ware continues in limited quantity, plain red ware is the dominant ceramic industry. The principal shapes in black slipped ware are bowls and dishes and bowls, dishes, basins and vases in red ware. Among the small finds terracotta discs appear for the first time while pottery discs continue to occur in limited quantity. Among the bone points some interesting shapes with punched circlet designs engraved on them have been noticed. Beads of glass, agate and terracotta, dabbers and balls and a terracotta figurine of horse constitute the small finds. Iron objects include a chisel and a nail. It seems that towards the end of period II, due to the menace of river Ghaghara the inhabitants moved to safer places like Mound-2 and Amauli village, to the north-east and due west of Mound-1 respectively.

Period III: Represented on Mound-2 this is charaterized by red ware, thick grey ware, black slipped ware, a few sherds of NBP ware and a kind of cord impressed pottery; the last one hitherto unrecorded from the sites of the middle Ganga plain, except in the Neolithic context at sites like Mahagara and Koldihwa in the Vindhyan ranges which, however, belongs to an altogether different tradition. Red ware is the principal ceramic industry and is divisible into three fabrics. viz., fine, medium and coarse. The fine fabric comprises the characteristic bowls with incurved or vertical featureless rim and a flat base, carinated *handi* with almost rounded base, reported from the middle of this period. Basins with nail headed externally collared rim, lipped basins, jars with splayed out rim and pear-shaped vase with collared rim were reported in the medium fabric. Cooking vessels were the principal type in coarse fabric. The grey ware is generally of coarse fabric with such types as medium sized dishes with pronounced incurved sides. Some sherds of this ware are of fine fabric as well and are comparable to those of the PGW of western U.P. and Haryana. The NBP ware sherds are limited in number and include dishes and bowls.

The structural remains of period III comprised mud-brick houses with associated mud floors and wattle-and-daub constructions in the lowest levels. Burnt lumps of clay with reed marks were met with. A noteworthy feature is the discovery of a storage jar buried under a house floor and a copper vessel placed in inverted position against this storage jar. Other antiquities of this period include copper and iron objects, beads, bangles, human figurines, discs, toy-cart wheels-all of terracotta and a copper coin from the upper levels of this period. It is a cast coin, square in shape. It bears an elephant, taurine, swastika and jayadhvaja on the obverse and tree-in-railing, taurine symbol, a three arched hill and a hollow cross on the reverse.

Charred grains recovered from this period include rice *(Oriza Sativa)*, barley *(Hordeum vulgare)* wheat *(Triticum aestivum* and *T. sphaerococcum)*, kodon millet *(Paspalum scrobiculatum)*, black gram *(Vigna mungo)*, green gram *(Vigna radiata)*, pea *(Pisum sativum)*, khesari *(Lathyrus sativus)* and sesame *(Sesamum indicum)*. Fruit-stone of jujube *(Ziziphus mauritiana)* and endocarp pieces of anwala *(Phyllanthus emblica)* have also been recovered.

A study of the mud plasters indicates that the earliest inhabitants of period III made use of bamboo for pole or beam and used reed plants of *Saccharum spontaneum* for their huts.

Impressions of some textile on the mud attached to a potsherd shows that the inhabitants of period III knew the spinning and weaving of cotton fabrics.

One charcoal sample from the upper levels of period IIIA (Sample No. B.S. 564) has been dated to 2200 ± 100 Y.B.P. while two others, both coming from the middle level of period IIIB (sample nos. B.S. 563 and 581) give the date of 2240 + 100 Y.B.P. and 2100 ± 100 Y.B.P., respectively.

Period IV was recorded from Mound-2. It is characterised by the absence of NBP ware, the dominant industry being the red ware represented by such shapes as bowls, dishes, vases, basins, sprinklers and lids. A complete specimen of sprinkler is an important discovery of Narhan excavations. Some of the sherds were decorated with stamped and incised designs. Another noteworthy find is a jar stand with three perforations. The structural remains were marked by the use of burnt bricks size 44x23x6 cm; 50x26x6 cm. A large room having two phases of construction, made of burnt bricks and having several post-holes cut into the burnt bricks ascribable to perhaps a third phase was exposed on Mound-2. A ring-well with inner diameter of 0.70 m and exposed upto 5 courses of rings in a depth of 0.80 m was found to the south-west of this room.

Among the small finds mention may be made of some terracotta figurines with exquisite workmanship. A terracotta plaque showing standing female figure with graceful body *bhanga* has been found. An identical piece has been reported from Rajghat (Narain & Agrawal, 1978). Several sealings one of which with legend *Shresthi kamalasya* palaeographically assignable to the Kushana period were obtained from the disturbed trench on the western slope of the mound. A charcoal sample from the lowest level of this period (sample No. B.S. 582) has been dated to 2200±100 Y.B.P.

Period V was represented by red ware with usual shapes reported from comparable levels of other sites. The structures of this period were found to be robbed by villagers. Mention may be made of a large number of star shaped figurines of mother-goddess all hand-made, from this period. A broken sealing with two letters *Dharma he,* assignable to the seventh century A.D. was recovered from this period. A notable find was a curious pot looking like an inverted dish-on-stand of red ware. As it comes from the disturbed trench on the western slope of Mound-2, its precise date is difficult to ascertain.

Pottery

The excavations yielded a rich repetoire of various ceramic industries. The entire ceramic asssemblage can be divided into five broad categories Black-and-red ware, Black Slipped-ware Grey ware, Northern Black Polished ware and Red ware. In the former four ceramic industries the entire pottery is wheel made while in the last one, hand made example is also met with in the case of basins and storage jars.

In period I BRW accounts for as much as 58% of the total ceramic assmblage while other wares are much less in quantity. A fairly good quantity of the sherds show burnishing. The shapes in BRW are mainly bowls, basins and vases. Dishes are altogether absent in this ware. A complete specimen of dish-on-stand has been reported from this site earlier. Two broken specimen of this type were picked up by us in the surface exploration. However this type has not been recorded in the limited dig so far. Shapewise the present complex is different than that found in western U.P. and northern Rajasthan at the type sites of Atranjikhera, Noh and Jodhoura. Basins with splayed out drooping rim and vase with flaring rim are prolific in Narhan while these types are absent at above mentioned sites. Similarly, nearly 23% of the medium and fine BRW is painted while the pottery at above sites is essentially plain. The paintings in BRW at Narhan constitute essentially linear pattern drawn in multiple brush technique in chocolate and dusty white colour; on the interior as well as the exterior of the pots. Some of the sherds bear diamond shape designs on the exterior of the pot in black colour. In some of the bowls the paintings can be seen all over the inner surface. The nearest parallel comes from Sohgaura. In the absence of any published drawings it is not possible to make any comparative study.

Black Slipped ware continues to occur in small quantity from period I but in the period II it becomes the main industry. This is mainly in fine and medium fabric and the shapes are bowls, dishes and miniature vessels. A new shape unreported from any other site is an elongate beaker. Basins are absent in this ware. A few pieces of BSW continue to occur in period III also but they are either in medium or coarse fabric. In the BSW of period I painted sherds are also met with in limited quantity and the paintings done in white pigment.

In the late levels of period III a few pieces of NBPW of steel blue variety have also been found in fine fabric.

Grey ware occurs in the upper levels of Period I, Period II and Period III. While the ware is mostly in fine and medium fabric, it is the coarse fabric which dominates in Period III. The main types are bowls and dishes with a few examples of medium size basins.

The red ware (including Red Slipped ware) is present right from the earliest layers of Period I. Here the characteristic features of this ware are bowls, basins and vases. The bowls are in extremely fine fabric. Small sized vases are typical of this period. A few four legged pots with perforation at the base have been found. The painted sherds have been found in this ware also. The painting is done in red ochre in multiple brush technique. The painting seems to be confined only to the bowls. In period II essentially the same types continue but in Period III we have a larger variety in the shapes of bowls, basins and vases. Fairly good quantity of the cord-impressed pottery has also been found in the earliest layers of Period III. Similar pottey found at other sites in this area has been assigned to Neolithic period. But at this site it is certainly of early historical period. One of the important features is that in this period we have many variants of Ahichchhatra 10A some of which may be the predecessors of this shape.

Carinated *handis* and knife-edged bowls are also met with in this period in large numbers.

The pottery of periods IV and V constitute essentially the same types commonly met with in Sunga-Kushana and Gupta periods on the sites of this region.

A Rare Object from Kosam

Jayantika Kala

Kosam representing ancient Kausambi, Capital of the Vatsa kingdom, has been a mine of rare and valuable antiquities. Most of these have gone into private collections and Museums.

In the Reserve Collection of the Allahabad Museum, there is a unique soft stone object which can be assigned to a period between the 3rd century B.C. and early 2nd century B.C. It was acquired by the Museum long ago and remains still unpublished.

The partly dome-shaped object which is flat at the bottom contains a crudely made nude female figure. It is executed in the same type of soft-stone found at Taxila, Ropar, Kausambi, Rajghat, Patna and Vaisali, which has been used for making artistic ring-stones. The style of the object under discussion, however, does not reflect work of a mature hand. The female figure is disproportionate and workmanship casual. The head is quite large and the face somewhat fearful. Her hair is drawn towards her back with a head-crest in the middle. Her extended left hand is raised and the right lowered. There is a rossette on either side of her hand and legs. Her navel is indicated by a perforated ringlet and her mount of Venus clear. Four rosettes are carved on the reverse of the object.

From the posture of her hands it is clear that the female is in a dance-posture, perhaps representing Mother Godess, a cult deity. A parallel type may be seen on a vertical stone panel discovered at Rajgir. It is divided in three compartments. The upper register shows a woman dancing to the tune of a harp played by a male figure. Her left hand is lowered and the right raised. She wears ear plaques and a sari [1]. Contrary to it, the figure in the Kausambi object is nude and devoid of ornaments. But a nude female figure can be seen on two fragmentary ringstone housed in the Bharat Kala Bhawan [2] and another in the Patna Museum [3].

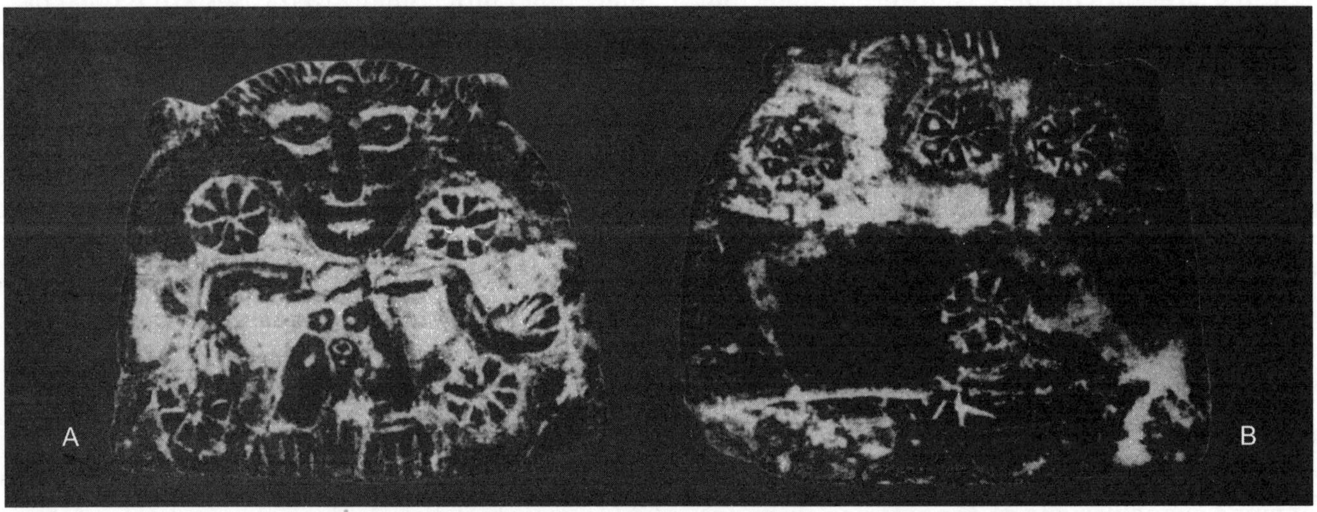

Stone sculpture from Kausambi: A. Obverse and B. Reverse.

1. *Indian Archaeology ; A Review 1962-63,* Pl- XII
2. *Chhavi,* Golden Jubilee Volume, Bharat Kala Bhawan, Varanasi, 1971, p.150
3. *J.B.R.S.,* Vol.XXVII, Parts 3-4, Pl X-3

A Note On "Archaeology Of Early Mediaeval Towns In Bengal"

B.N. Mukherjee

Dr. V.K. Thakur has recently published in the pages of the *Puratattva* an interesting article entitled "Archaeology of Early Mediaeval Towns in Bengal".[1] In that paper he has tried to establish that archaeological excavations at Chandraketurgarh (24 Parganas, West Bengal), Goswamikhanda (Burdwan district, West Bengal), Rajabadidanga (Murshidabad district, West Bengal), and Bangarh (West Dinajpur district, West Bengal) suggest that they survived in the Pala period for their association with religion and that they were "non-commercial townships under the aegis of a political authority".[2]

We like to point out that excavations at Bangarh, carried out by the Calcutta University, clearly proved that it was a regular city (not a temple-city) and that one of its prosperous phases corresponded to the Pala period.[3] The city was known as Kotivarsha and later as Devikota (Diwkot of Mulsim writers).[4]

A small area was excavated at Goswamikhanda[5] to detect the real character of the habitation in the whole locality.[6]

Similarly, only a small portions of the vast area of Chandraketurgarh (as indicated by the remnants of the rampart wall) have been excavated. Nevertheless, numerous objects of utilitarian and decorative value, found here by archaeologists and local people, indicate that it might have been a regular urban centre. There is nothing to prove that religion became the basis of its survival in the Pala age. At least the presence of a shrine (referred to by Thakur) cannot characterise the whole area as the site of a temple-city. In fact, the excavators themselves have admitted that only the relevant part of the mound, where the shrine has been unearthed, "was perhaps the centre of religious activity in the periods VII and VIII" (i.e., from the third to the sixth and from the seventh to the tenth century A.D.).[7] It is inexpedient to see in the character of a building the nature of habitation of the whole area.

We should also remember that no urban site can be purely non-commercial (even if it grows around a religious institution), since daily necessities of the local people require commercial transactions. The discoveries of seals of merchants at the site of a monastery at Rajabadidanga[8] may allude to either commercial transactions in a place dedicated to religion or at least to its connection with some traders.

The ruins unearthed at Rajabadidanga represent the monastery of Raktamrittika.[9] The legend on a number of seals found here refers to "the community of the noble monks of the Great Vihara of or at the illustrious Raktamrittika.[10] According to Hsuan-tsang, the monastery of Loch'a-mo-chi (i.e., Raktamrittika) was situated near the town of Karnasuvarna.[11] So the locality of Rajabadidanga was in the neighbourhood of a town, but itself was not a regular town.

It appears from the above observations that V.K. Thakur is absolutely wrong in taking religion as the basis of survival of Bangarh or Chandraketurgarh and in considering Rajabadidanga as the site of a township. It is also surprising that while he wants to determine the character of early mediaeval towns in 'Bengal', he has confined himself to West Bengal only, and has not taken into account the Bangladesh area of 'Bengal'. He has completely ignored the famous city site at Mainamati, which, together with its religious establishments, continued to flourish in the Pala-Chandra period.[12] The city was known as Devaparvata.[13]

Pundranagara (Mahasthana in the Bogra district of Bangladesh) continued to be an urban area in the period concerned.[14] Ramavati was a metropolis in the later Pala period.[15] Vikramapura (near Dacca, in Eastern Bangladesh) was an important urban centre, where one of the victorious camps of the Senas was located.[16] It appears from the *Tabaqat-i-Nasiri* that Lakhnawati (Lakshmanavati = Gauda = Gaur in the Malda district), Diw-kot (Deokot or Bangarh in the West Dinajpur district) and Nudiah (Nadiya in the Nadiya district) were three other important cities of West Bengal.[17]

Thus there was no unusual dearth of regular cities in early mediaeval 'Bengal'. There may have been religious establishments in these urban settlements; but there is no evidence to prove that they existed only as centres of religious activities. On the other hand, as we have shown elsewhere, some of them were great centres of commercial activities.[18] 'Bengal' in the Pala-Sena period witnessed internal, transit and external trade.[19]

No doubt, archaeological excavations in West Bengal and Bangladesh have not yet laid bare in great number cities or towns datable to the period concerned. But here the fault lies with the archaeologists, Archaeological Survey of India and the departments of Archaeology in West Bengal and Bangladesh and not with the ruins of urban settlements. Impressive mounds and available archaeological remains, like those at Mangalkot and Amavati (West Bengal), allude to large city-sites of the period concerned. They still await regular digging by professional archaeologists.[20]

REFERENCES

1. *Puratattva*, 1980-81, No. 12 pp. 140-144.

2. *Ibid.*, p. 144.

3. K.G. Goswami, *Excavation at Bangarh*, Calcutta, 1948 pp. 5-9 and 38-39.

4. *Ibid.*, *Tabaqat-i-Nasiri*, XX, 5 and 8; H.G. Baverty, *The Tabakat-i-Nasiri*, Vol. I, reprint, New Delhi 1970, pp. 584-586.

5. *Indian Archaeology 1963-64 — A Review*, pp. 60-61.

6. *Ibid.*

7. *Indian Archaeology 1961-62 — A Review*, p. 62. [Take the case of present-day Varanasi, Allahabad, Mathura]. etc. (ed.)

8. *Indian Archaeology 1968-69 — A Review*, p. 43.

9. S.R. Das, *Rajabadidanga, 1962*, Calcutta, 1963, pp. 23f, 43 and 56-57.

10. *Ibid.*, pp. 56-58.

11. Hsuan-tsang, *Hsi-yu-chi*, Chuan XX; T. Watters, *On Yuan Chwang's Travels in India*, Vol. II, London, 1904, pp. 191-192.

12. B.M. Morrison, *Lalmai, A Cultural Centre of East Bengal*, Seattle and London, pp. 120f.

13. D.C. Sircar, *Epigraphic Discoveries in East Pakistan*, Calcutta, 1973, pp. 23, 24 and 65f. Devaparvata is referred to in detail in two epigraphs.

14. N. Ahmed, *Mahasthan*, Dacca, 1975, pp. 24f; B.M. Morrison, *op. cit.*, pp. 124-125.

15. Sandhyakaranandi, *Ramacharita*, III, 32f.

16. N.G. Majumdar, *Inscriptions of Bengal*, Vol. III, Rajshahi, 1929, pp. 63, 73, 86, etc.; B.M. Morrison, *op. cit.*, pp. 122f.

17. *Tabaqat-i-Nasiri*, XX, 5 and 8; H.G. Raverty, *op. cit.*, pp. 554, 559 (fn.2), 584-586. Lakhnawati is referred to in several manuscripts of the *Tabaqat-i-Nasiri* as Lakhn-or (H.G. Raverty, *op.cit.*, p. 585) (*Lakshmananagara » Lakkhana + nagara » Lakhana + nayara » Lakhnayara Lakhnor).*

18. See our article published in the *Indian Museum Bulletin*, 1982.

19. *Ibid.*

20. Even the excavated area of an archaeological site is not always coterminus with or even reasonably proportionate to the locality itself, the span of which is indicated by surrounding mounds.

Book Reviews

R.C. Gaur **Excavations at Atranjikhera—Early Civilization of the Upper Ganga Basin:** Centre for Advanced Study, Department of History, Aligarh Muslim University— Motilal Banarsidas, Delhi (1983).

This is the first authentic and consolidated report on the excavations at the mound of Atranjikhera in Etah district, U.P., begun from 1962 first and carried on in over seven seasons from 1964 by the team of archaeologists headed by Prof. R.C. Gaur of the Ancient History and Archaeology Department, Aligarh Muslim University. The inspiration for this sustained work, doubtless, came from the distinguished historian, scholar and statseman, Professor Nurul Hasan, Professor Emeritus, Aligarh Muslim University and currently India's Ambassador to the Soviet Union.

Atranjikhera excavations have supplemented and to some extent supplanted the solitary and exclusive importance of the excavations at Hastinapura more than two decades ago by Professor B.B. Lal, a doyen among the archaeologists in India today and a former Director General of the Archaeological Survey of India. It has projected effectively the cultures prior to the advent of the Painted Grey Ware-using people (recently claimed as the likely bearers of the Vedic legacy by Prof. Lal himself) in the first half of the second millennium B.C., in the form of the Ochre-colored Pottery users and plain Black-and-Red Ware users, not to mention the gift of ^{14}C date for probably the earliest known context of use of iron in Upper India in the western Ganga basin, coeval with the Painted Grey Ware-using levels of the site.

The problems which these excavations sought to answer were many, and the issues raised as a sequel to these investigations are many more. Suffice it to say, however, that the picture of cultural devolutions in the western Ganga valley is ever more clear and promising than before, and would help in establishing the antecedent matrix of cultural manifestations of human communities in this zone with plausible nexus with what transpired in the late Harappan stages in the neighbouring Haryana to the west and the southwesterly and southerly nuclei of coeval movements. Indeed excavations of the sites of the Indus Civilization and its aftermath in the areas west of Yamuna, in the Banas valley and in the Malwa plateau, would have seen a fitting foil in the results of Atranjikhera. They would be posing seriously the interactions and movements in this period of great cultural displacements and shifts. This had led also to the consolidation of the Ganga valley civilization in the whole of the first millennium B.C. They are thus pregnant with assessment—potential towards the cultural efflorescence, thrust and growth into what is claimed as the Indian culture today. The value of Atranjikhera excavations is, thus, not only adventitious, but also complementary to the culture-spectrum of the Chalcolithic phase of Upper India.

The report, leaning heavily as it is expected to be, on the index value of pottery cultures, besides antiquities and stone-using traditions in the early phases marginally, has been painstakingly collected and documented, but rather briefly analysed under each chapter, particularly of Periods I —III, whereafter Period IV of the N.B.P. phase follows in mid-Iron Age, as day follows night. The most tantalising part of the excavations pertains, however, to the first three periods which, but for Period I, but even including it, as found on the ground, occur as colonisations of a limited part of this very large mound, as reflected in the lenticular depositional formations of culture deposits, not fully relevent to all parts of the mound. This is indeed to be taken as one of the gifts of archaeological investigations and firmly place physically the mechanics of the concerned culture inceptions and inter-relations prior to Period IV which is evenly spread throughout the mound. Breaks of occupation have been visualised as 'fill', as it is called, 'containing Ocher-coloured pottery and Black-and-Red ware sherds seen just below the regular Black-and-Red ware deposit' may imply anything, it may be an overlap rather than a break when taken as due to the process of levelling of the ground, as done, but the Black-and-Red ware people; and may mean that both the people might have been together at some part of time. Be this as it may, it is the physical profile of the tip of the mound containing these two successive early cultures that is visually eloquent and suggestive of the fresh colonisation of the second Period people over those of Period I which was an entrenched cultivational community which seemingly sought an adventitious water table for the operations and was deliberately occupying a basin of the river front. The rather limited area of about 400 square metres where these significant activities of Period II were focussed on also underscores village communities thriving on river propinquity, against a forested background. The excavator has clearly distinguished, however, the hard brownish earth and clay composition of Period I and the burnt, ashy nature of that of Period II with remnants of kilns, domestic hearths and big pits. Seemingly, thus, the nature of the activity of Period II was truly habitational, while it was agricultural in Period I, dealing with rice and barley. The problems connected with rice-eating zone distribution with that of the wheat and barley-using ones, especially where they met, is of extreme importance in the ultimate analysis for western Ganga basin, taking note of the chiefly wheat and barley-using propensities of the Harappan culture.

The pottery of Period I of Atranjikhera is considered as having much similarity with that of Bahadarabad, Hastinapura, Ambkheri and other Ocher-coloured pottery sites, although pots of Harappan affinity are found missing here. The site being located further down the *antarvedi* and the links between the Harappan and the Ocher-coloured ware people having been established better on the north end of the *doab* around Saharanpur district and the neighbouring Punjab area where Bargaon, Bahadarabad and Ambkheri are located, one may venture the suggestion that in areas south of Hastinapura, Rajpur Parsu,etc., on the *doab,* there is less likelihood of Harappan links and, contrariwise, the Ochre–coloured ware of the southerly sites are likely to be of anterior chronological position. Saipai was perhaps the farthest southern limit in Uttar Pradesh of this ware. If so, one could posit that the central region of this ware could have been the southerly districts like Etah. The excavator had, indeed, tried to consider three distinctive groups of the sites of the Ware: (i) those with Harappan influence, (ii) Harappan sites with Ochre Coloured Ware influence, and (iii) genuine Ochre-coloured Ware sites. It is obvious that the former two are liable to be in the more northerly districts of Meerut, Muzaffarnagar, Saharanpur and Dehradun in the *doab*—which is what we have argued above. It is found that incised decorations, so characteristic of sites like Lal Qila, Atranjikhera and Saipai are unknown at Ambkheri where limited Harappan traits are however present. Perhaps the 'Pre-Harappan' trait of the horizontal black painted bands traditionally continued in the upper *doab* chiefly after the disapperance of the Harappan culture proper.

As regards the cultural content of the early periods of Atranjikhera, it would seem appropriate to designate them functionally as early agricultural Copper age, truly Chalcolithic phase and early Iron Age phase, respectively. If considered so, it would be apparent how only in Period II external movements of the Black-and-Red ware using people had been witnessed at the site, and the arrival of the Painted Grey ware using people in Period III could be later than that of the upper *doab* sites like Hastinapura. The main sections (fig. 6 and 26) seem to indicate that Period II was eroded by considerable disturbances and cross-bedded layers indicative of unsettled conditions, before the firm horizontal layers (from 48 upwards) could be seen of Period IV. Does this mean that the large scale Ganga floods which destroyed Hastinapura during its Painted Grey Ware period had also been felt at Atranjikhera (which is on a tributary system), and N.B.P. occupation on a firm footing had been also delayed ? The sedate N.B.P. layers seem to belong to middle stage of that culture. Professor Lal's recent catagorization of the pottery types of the N.B.P. period into three distinctive diagnostic stages are relevant here, and the analysis of the signigicant types like the carinated handi and the so-called Ahichchhatra 10a type and others could be statistically examined with advantage from the documented material in the report of Atranjikhera. In fact, excavator has himself divided the Period IV into four phases (A-D) which seems to reveal that Phase A is in fact the period of erosion of the site and has mostly elements of both pottery and diagnostic antiquity types of Period III, and only phases C and D pertain to the firm and fully established Period IV stages. This aspect could be made to yield more substantial inferences from a detailed study of the data already documented in the report under review.

The significant show of the microlithic cores and flakes of Period II do not appear to have been given its due in the report. This section (p.119) is somewhat meagre, though the excavator has referred to the raw material occurrence as likely to have been imported from the Sawai Madhopur tract of Rajasthan, based on geological report. These microlithic cores have also been metioned as having their chipping done transversely (fig. 40). What seems to have been missed is that this is a characteristic of the 'crested-guiding—ridge' technique, to which indeed the collection from Period II would mostly pertain. These are dated in the report as of the time bracket of 1450-1200 B.C. pertaining to Period II. We may note that the occurrence of these 'crested-guiding-ridge' types could be the culture-residue of the Rajasthan and Central Indian Chalcolithic, coeval with the Black-and-Red ware, as seen at Navdatoli, Maheshwar and the Banas valley, and may lead to the inference that the penetration of the Chalcolithic culture traits into Atranjikhera zone would have left the core and flake traditions in a rather degenerate stage. It is also to be noted that Period I is devoid of such cores and flakes.

The excavator is legitimately holding that the three early culture periods of the site are not *in situ*, evolutions of the *same* people by borrowals, but the successive occupations of the site by three distinctive communities, of which the earliest would alone be indigenous but had virtually become effete by Period II. Thus, the Chalcolithic shift registered in Period II was from the south and south-west. Similarly, the shift of Painted Grey Ware-using people into the site in Period III was from the northern part of the *doab*. The total disappearance of any stone flakes, etc., in Period III would show that the emergent impact of iron technology would have effectively killed the stone tool usages.

It is legitimate that the ethnic labelling of the cultures as Pre-Aryan and Aryan could not be resisted and are raised in the context of the excavation report. But it is unavailing to link them with the Vedic culture; rather, the emphasis should be on the fact that a geographical and zonal dichotomy of the two wares, namely the Black-and-Red Ware and the Painted Grey Ware exists wherein the former did *not* pertain to the region where Vedas are held as having been composed, on literary evidence, leaving the rest to further possibilities on the basis of true occupational material traits revealed in excavations. (Archaeological and literary evidence would necessarily run on parallel lines, being of two *genres*, and until correlations on occupational basis could be seen, and links forged, linguistic tags can be avoided). The long history of the Painted Grey Ware in north-western India and Pakistan in Haryana, Punjab, north-east Rajasthan, Lakhio Pir in Sind, at Harappa, in Baluchistan, in Sistan, at Shah Tepe, as listed and referred to by the excavator, would give us enough hope to hold on to likely further archaeological break-through in this regard, though the chances are that the material remnants of the Vedic culture in daily use might have proved flimsy and ephemeral. Meanwhile, we are not grudging to the excavator his desire to discuss literary data, as done by him.

It would be churlish to point out the minor deficiencies in the report, like the absence of the markings of the excavated trenches in the survey plan of the site (fig.1). As no clear references are given to their location in the text also and a business-like short description of the Cuttings would have greatly enhanced the value of the report, the comment should not be unwelcome.

The book is printed and designed in a manner that would be most useful to students and scholars alike, with copious illustrations and running documentation of the pottery cultures and juxtaposed drawings. This is surely a major contribution to our understanding of what happened on the threshold of history.

K.V. Soundara Rajan

S.P. Shukla, **Sculptures and Terracottas in the Archaeological Museum, Kurukshetra University,** pages 77, Plates I-VIII, 1983. Published by Registrar, Kurukshetra University, Kurukshetra, Price Rs. 62/-

The monograph is a well documented work, embodying the works of art from Thanesvar, Pehowa, Kaithal, Sirsa, Pinjora and Nauranga-bad in Haryana, and Sanghol, Sunet and Ajarm in Punjab. It is preceeded by an introduction in two parts : i) stone sculptures attributable to early post-Gupta and medieval periods, and ii) early historic terracottas. Almost each entry is accompanied by an illustration given at the end. It has also a classified list of the museum specimens.

The stone sculptures comprise Vaishnava, Saiva, Sakta and Jain imagery besides some architectural components of the religious edifices. The image in plate XXV. 2 is more appropriately *uruh-ghanta,* originally forming a component of the *samavarana,* rather than *uruh-sringa.*

The terracotta figurines of mother goddesses, Mahishamardini, *Salabhanjika, Vamanika, dvarapala,* narrative plaques and animal figurines such as the elephant, ram, horse, deer, bear and reptiles, and birds have also been included. Amongst the miscellaneous finds mention may be made of the potter's dabbers, wheels and votive tanks. The monograph is useful, despite the unsatisfactory plates.

P.K. Trivedi

V.S. Agrawala, **Varansai Seals and Sealings** Edited by Dr. P.K. Agrawala, pp. 48, plates I-XX, 1984. Published by Prithvi Prakashan, Varansai, Price Rs. 175/-

Published as No. XXVIII of the 'Indian Civilization Series, this book is a collection of the notes of the late Prof. V.S. Agrawala written during the early fifties. The notes are edited and arranged into two parts by P.K. Agrawala. The first half is devoted to the study of seals and sealings from Rajghat, representing the ancient settlement of present-day Varanasi and an incomplete note in Hindi: the second half deals with the Gupta seals and sealings.

The seals included in the first chapter are attributed to various religions, educational institutions and kings, minsters, officers, guilds and many others. Some tablets reveal the names of Indo-Greek rulers, and Greek deities, viz. Athena, Nike, Herecles and Apollo. Several hundred tablets bearing the name 'Dhanadeva' were recovered from Rajghat. Dhanadeva was the successor of Abhaya and has been identified with the Kausambi ruler whose coins are also well known. A clay seal, bearing *(Dha) nadeva* in the characters of first century, has also been recovered from Sringaverapura. The clay sealings detailed in a separate chapter are at present lodged in the Bharat Kala Bhawan, Varanasi; Municipal Museum, Allahabad; State Museum, Lucknow and National Museum, New Delhi. They were recovered from the digs carried out during the forties by the Railway Department and subsequently by the Archaeological Survey of India. The paper entitled 'Rajghat aṣ Prsta Mitti Ki Muharon Ka Ek Adhyayana' in Hindi is incomplete.

The second half of the volume includes 382 tablets assignable to princes, rulers, ministers, officers and offices, 'Srenis'; Vedic academies; Brahmanical and Buddhist sects, etc. all dating from the first century B.C. to the late Gupta period. P.K. Agrawal has deciphered 119 more seals in consultation with Shri Krishna Deva.

The book supplements K.K. Thaplayal's *Studies in Ancient Indian Seals* and Swami Omanand Saraswati's *Haryana Ke Prachina Mudranka.*

P.K. Trivedi